World of Hunger

JONATHAN POWER
& ANNE~MARIE HOLENSTEIN

WORLD OF HUNGER

A strategy for survival

Temple Smith·London

First published in Great Britain 1976
by Maurice Temple Smith Ltd
37 Great Russell Street, London WC1
© 1976 Jonathan Power & Anne-Marie Holenstein
Typesetting by Red Lion Setters, London
ISBN 0 85117 0978 cased
0 85117 0951 paperback
Printed in Great Britain by
Billings Ltd, Guildford and London

Contents

Famine is something quite peculiar. It concentrates all effort and thought and feeling on one thing. It makes everyone a frustrated glutton. In a famished town, as in a cheap restaurant, there is always a flavour of food in the air. Everybody brooding on food makes a smell which hangs about them like the smell of gravy and cabbage about a dirty table-cloth. Somehow famine goes beyond hunger and puts in each face a kind of lewdness; a kind of grey unwholesome longing. People's white gums and mouldering flesh suggest rather a consuming disease like leprosy than appetite. They seem diseased, even evil, rather than pathetic. Their eyes are greedy and restless, and linger greedily, it some-times seems, on one another's bodies. Their skin gets unnaturally dry and their breath parched and stale like dry air in a cellar.

Malcolm Muggeridge, *Winter in Moscow* (London 1934) quoted in *The Conquest of Famine,* W.R. Aykroyd (London 1974)

1 Introduction

This book is about hunger — an age-old subject that has been with us since the serpent tempted Adam and Eve to pluck the apple. But it is not a book that seeks to play upon the emotions with a recital of the well-worn facts about starving children and emaciated bodies. Rather it is an attempt to come to grips with the fundamental factors involved in putting the curse of famine and hunger behind us once and for all.

This is an ambitious exercise, but the situation we confront is now so critical, threatening to engulf whole continents whose stability and destiny are closely interwoven with our own, that we have no other choice but to set about the task.

Yet the historical precedents are not encouraging.

In 917 a contemporary chronicle of the Kashmir famine records that the land became covered with bones until it resembled a vast burial ground, while the king and his ministers, far from attempting to relieve suffering, amassed riches by selling grain at a high price.

When the great Irish famine got under way, 130 years ago, Charles Trevelyan, the Treasury civil servant responsible for famine policy, refused to allow the procurement of home cereals for relief because it would 'disturb the market'. In Bernard Shaw's *Man and Superman,* the returned Irish American, Malone, insists on calling the famine 'the starvation'.

> 'Me father died of starvation in the black '47. Maybe you've heard of it?'
> 'The famine?'
> 'No, the starvation. When a country is full of food and exporting it, there can be no famine. Me father was starved dead and I was starved out to America in me mother's arms.'

7

When the Bengal famine of 1943 began — the worst this century — the India Office, under L.S. Amery, refused to admit its existence, preferring the euphemism 'food shortage'. A government commission, charged with finding why over two million people died, later found that 'it lay in the power of the government of Bengal, by bold, resolute and well conceived measures at the right time to have largely prevented the tragedy of the famine as it actually took place.'

Famine and hunger in one important sense are more easy to solve today than they were in previous times. Man now has the technology and the resources to quickly achieve the most ambitious of targets, witness President Kennedy's bold decision to put a man on the moon within ten years. Yet for all man's new potential we appear to have constructed political systems that make an attack on poverty more difficult than it was in past ages.

Above all, we have the legacy of colonialism. For a large part of the last four hundred years, the major European powers have been moulding the peoples of Africa and Asia and Latin America to their own needs: encouraging economies, however lacking they were in technological expertise, to throw off the internal self-sufficiency they once had. And not just self-sufficiency in a productive sense but self-sufficiency socially where the little that people had was often shared reasonably equitably. Instead of this, they were encouraged, persuaded, enticed and sometimes compelled to orientate their economies in a quite different direction. They were seen too often as suppliers of raw materials for *our* growth. Development in the Third World during the eighteenth, nineteenth and early twentieth centuries, such as it was, proceeded outwards from the ports. The plantation, the mining and the cash crop economy were introduced. Taxes were often used not so much as a revenue source for central government, but as a way of compelling peasants to grow cash crops or work in the mines. The slow attrition of the food production system had begun, a process which was to gradually gather speed until in the last twenty years we have seen the complete demoralisation of the countryside and the increased attraction of the city, despite the fact that well over half its

8

inhabitants live in shanty towns or their equivalent.

The idea that the rural community had a self-sufficient potential of its own, albeit at a higher economic level than the one prevailing, did not interest the colonial powers. Too often when they found indigenous rural industry, they set out to ruin it, seeing in it the seeds of competition with the new industrialisation back home. In India where before British rule there had been a thriving textile industry, the British introduced a system of tariffs and taxes in order to encourage its liquidation. From 1800 to 1850 under the influence of the British Raj there evolved a whole network of elaborate mercantilist provisions whose purpose was to increase the exports of British goods to India. India's exports to Britain were prohibited by tariff walls. Within India British textiles had to pay only a small 3½ per cent ad valorem import duty, while local manufacturers and traders in Indian textiles had to pay from 6 to 18 per cent ad valorem inland transit duties.

Today, although colonialism only exists in odd enclaves, it is not easy for developing countries to break away from its legacy. Educational systems, established by colonial governments, stress the urban culture, particularly its more superficial characteristics — ambition, status, consumer satisfaction. The countryside, agriculture and the old conventions are regarded as inferior and unrewarding. And in the town, the most advanced technology of the west too often is welcomed unthinkingly. Unemployment and underemployment may be the common condition but the fascination and prestige that is found in highly developed capital intensive technology takes precedence. And this technology leads to a kind of economic and political union that ties the developing countries to the West's umbilical cord even more tightly than nineteenth-century gunboat colonialism ever did.

As long as western ideas of material satisfaction, instant reward, urban pleasure are being fed into an unsophisticated populace, it is going to be impossible to reorientate the Third World back to its most precious and important asset — the land. This is not the call of romantic pastoral reformers who believe all virtue lies in the land. Rather it is where the harsh

9

facts of a near impossible situation point us. The future
wellbeing of the Third World lies in its peasant farmers.
Only if this asset is realised will the Third World gain the
power, independence and dignity it strives after.

2 The bottleneck

For a number of years now, experts have spoken of a threatening world food crisis mainly because of the population explosion. But because of overflowing supermarkets and regularly increasing purchasing power in the industrialised countries this threat seemed extremely theoretical and pessimistic; and meanwhile in developing nations the thesis was refuted by the Green Revolution. In India the state of Bihar, which in 1965 and 1966 was still suffering from a catastrophic famine, was able to become an exporter of grain and could for the first time build up reserve stocks.

But then in 1971 and 1972, bad weather caused failed harvests in the Soviet Union, China, India, Australia, the Sahel and South-East Asia. For the first time in twenty years there was a fall in the world production of wheat, legumens and rice, a fall of some thirty-three million tons. This 4 per cent drop in world production set off a crisis that was felt throughout the world. Previous optimism about the world food situation gave way to violently pessimistic forecasts.

Contrary to the case in previous years of bad harvests, the Soviet Union did not try to overcome its problems by tightening its belt and reducing its demand for animal fodder by reducing cattle stocks. Instead the Soviet Union entered the world market as a major buyer. United States wheat stocks, which had for many years served as a buffer against crisis situations, sank from forty-nine million tons in 1971/72 to twenty-nine million tons in 1973. So by the middle of 1973 the world grain stocks were in the same situation as they had been twenty years earlier. Yet in that time the world population had increased by one half. Remaining stock represented reserves for thirty-seven days. In 1961 stocks had covered world needs for ninety-five days.[1]

As a result of the shortages, export prices doubled between 1972 and 1973. Hardest hit were the lower-income brackets

11

who were already paying out up to 80 per cent of their earnings for food. A doubling of prices meant for them a halving in the purchase of food. Nobody knows how many hundreds of thousands of people in South-East Asia, Africa and Latin America starved to death as a result. The already grave situation was made even worse by the disappearance from Peruvian coastal waters of the anchovy fish. In earlier years an average of ten million cubic tons had been caught annually and processed into high-protein animal feedstuff. Now the market swung to soya. Soya-bean prices rapidly accelerated to five times their original level and the United States, with two thirds of world production and 90 per cent of the world market, imposed a temporary ban on exports.

Good harvests in 1973 prevented a catastrophe but the situation remained acute. Prices continued to rise. For a time wheat prices were four times up on the previous year's, maize trebled its price and by March 1974 Thai rice had risen to over four times its normal price. Scarcity was not the only cause, but also monetary uncertainty, inflation and a higher degree of short-term credits. In addition there was a sharp step up in speculative grain buying.

The United States, Australia and Canada, the world's biggest grain producers, could have avoided the situation of dwindling stocks. In 1967 the USA and Canada introduced measures to reduce production because they were afraid of saturating the market with grain, so lowering the price. This proved a vital mistake for the hungry millions elsewhere in the world. Had those fields under cultivation in 1967 remained in production, there would have been some hundred million extra tons of grain in 1972. This would have meant that price rises would have been much less dramatic. By 1973 the security of world nutrition depended almost entirely upon the new harvest.

Another problem for the developing countries is a general shortage of fertilisers. The existing means of manufacturing fertilisers can hardly keep up with rising demand. Moreover, the increase in oil prices has had a corresponding effect on the price of fertilisers. In many developing countries fertilisers

12

are unobtainable or too expensive at the time they are needed.

As a result of the steep price rises for oil-dependent products and foodstuffs between 1972 and 1974, the non-oil-producing developing countries have fallen into chronic balance of payment difficulties which they cannot get out of without external assistance. Just for essential products for basic existence they had to pay a total of fifteen thousand million dollars more in 1974 than the year before. In 1974 the sum total of development aid was 8.6 thousand million dollars. This amount was not enough to pay for half the oil deficit, let alone support crucial development plans.

Not since the Second World War had the security of the world's food supplies been so critically dependent on one harvest, as it has been in 1974 and 1975-1976. If all had gone well in 1974, that is to say if the high-risk factor, the weather, had been favourable, then price conditions would have stabilised somewhat and reserves could have been rebuilt. But this did not happen. The world food harvest for only the second time in twenty-five years fell back on the previous year's level. The reasons for this were frost and drought in North America and floods in the Indian subcontinent. The available quantities could have covered worldwide demand, but the rich countries proved that they were not prepared to reduce their consumption for the benefit of those worse off. The injustice in all rationing systems began to function: namely the indirect rationing through price which makes food unobtainable for people in those countries with little money to spare. Bangladesh, Sri Lanka and parts of India were badly hit by famine in 1974. Even worse hit by the lingering famine were the poorest dispersed regions of the Third World. Many of the relief measures came too late to save people from starvation.

The situation began to ease a little in early 1975. Grain prices began to fall on the world market as the recession cut purchasing power in the West, and the Soviet Union and China reduced their orders. In addition the 1975 crop was good. Yet this optimism did not solve everything. The FAO (Food and Agriculture Organisation) repeated what was true in 1973, 1974 and 1975: the world's supplies still depended on the next harvest. Man is now living from hand to mouth. And the second great Russian grain deal rammed the message of uncertainty home. Wheat prices threatened to break previous record levels.

But for all that, the inhabitants of the rich countries have become accustomed to living with the 'world food crisis'. What does it mean to the individual? In industrialised countries with high living standards it just means paying a bit more for food. The fact that grain supplies are extremely low hardly registers at all. To anyone who has money to buy these things with, life continues its normal course. What then does the world food crisis mean? Its origins and symptoms are much broader than just the bottleneck in the world grain market, and its solutions even more complex. These complex interlocking factors will be looked at in the following chapters.

3 Why is there a food shortage today?

The present bottleneck in food supply is not just the responsibility of the developing countries, because they are producing more people than food. The inhabitants of the western countries are often too quick to forget their own contribution to the crisis — the fact that as wealth increases people consume more food. The average yearly increase of thirty million tons in cereal production is not primarily absorbed by the growing numbers of hungry people. Nearly one third of that increased output goes in meeting the demand for more refined foodstuff from the increasingly affluent. In the poorer countries of the world there is an annual per capita supply of 400 pounds of corn. In the United States and Canada it is nearer 2,000 pounds. (And these figures do not indicate the internal distribution of food in these countries.)

An average North American needs five times more land, water and fertiliser than the average Indian, Nigerian or Colombian. According to Professor Jean Mayer of Harvard University, the same amount of food that is needed for 210 million Americans could feed 1.5 thousand million Chinese. Conversely, René Dumont makes the reproach that agricultural production would not even meet the demands of one thousand million people if they all wanted to live at the United States' standard of living. These figures however do not mean that an average American eats five times as much as an Indian. Of the 2,000 pounds of cereals that are available for him the American only eats some 150 pounds directly as bread, confectionery, breakfast cereals, flour products etc. The remaining 1,850 pounds are used as animal foodstuff to produce the meat, milk, cheese and eggs whose share in the diet increases sharply as income grows.

In contrast millions of Indians, who have an average of only 400 pounds of cereal at their disposal, have to use the whole amount directly in order to satisfy minimum energy needs. They cannot afford meat, which could reduce the protein deficit in their diets. The same trend emerges all over the world. He who earns more eats more meat and hence demands an increased supply of cereal, since to produce 1 pound of beef, 6½ pounds of cereal in the form of animal fodder are needed. To produce 1 pound of pork, 3½ pounds of cereal are needed, and 2 pounds of cereal for 1 pound of chicken. Even more serious is the mal-use of protein. In the USA it is estimated that 21 pounds of pure protein in cattle fodder are used to produce only 1 pound of beef or veal. To produce 1 pound of pork, 8.5 pounds of pure protein are used, and 5½ pounds of protein for 1 pound of chicken.

Between 1962 and 1972 the total production of foodstuffs increased by 2.7 per cent a year. The world demand for feed grains rose much faster — 6.3 per cent a year between 1961 and 1963 and 1969 and 1971. In total the rich countries required 620 million tons of grain in 1973. More than half of this, 374 million tons, was fed to cattle. In the 1960s 78 per cent of the total grain fed to cattle was utilised by the United States.

It is only recently that the USA, the world's biggest meat-consuming country, appeared to reach its saturation limit. Consumption of beef in the USA doubled between 1942 and 1972 from 55 pounds per head to 117 pounds. Chicken consumption almost trebled over the same period (from 18 to 51 pounds).

A long list of important industrialised countries ranging from Britain through to Scandinavia, Western Europe, Eastern Europe, the Soviet Union and Japan have now brought their living standards up to the level of the United States in the 1940s. With living standards still rising a pattern of meat consumption similar to that in the USA can be expected. For example in Japan the per capita consumption of meat increased by 50 per cent between 1969 and 1972.

The cereal purchases of the Soviet Union in 1973 must be seen in this context. These purchases have now become the most crucial factor in the current food crisis (see page 184). With a drastic cutback in meat production the USSR could have balanced out the bad harvest. But in 1972-73 for the first

16

Table 1: Direct and indirect grain consumption per capita income, selected countries. [1] Source: Food and Agriculture Organization, Food Balance Sheets, 1964-66 Average (Rome 1971).

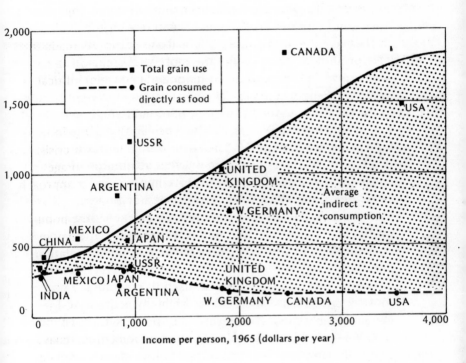

Income per person, 1965 (dollars per year)

time they decided against this form of crisis management and instead bought one fifth of the total United States wheat harvest. The shortage caused by this drove prices up and once more it was the developing countries who felt the effects, either directly because of dwindling food reserves or indirectly through a drop in deliveries of cereals through the American Food Aid Programme PL 480 (see chapter 5).

The second report of the Club of Rome argues that: 'Overproduction has become the most vital competitor with hunger in the struggle to maintain a constant supply of food . . . . People in industrial countries can hardly contribute to the relief of the food situation, since in attempting to do so they would have to drastically alter their lifestyle and their typical dietary patterns.'[2] The crisis in short is not the result of a lack of resources but of an uneven distribution of such resources. The Cocoyoc declaration, composed in October 1974 by leading Third World politicians and academics, states that 'there could hardly be a more vivid example of what one might call the overconsumption of the wealthy nations contributing directly to the underconsumption of the world's poor.'[3]

Seen in this perspective, we all need to redefine our goals, to work out new development strategies, new life-styles, including more modest patterns of consumption among the rich. We should be looking for those development strategies that will help the affluent countries to find more human patterns of life, less exploitative of nature, of others, of themselves. Sicco L. Mansholt, the former Dutch Minister of Agriculture and former President of the Common Market Commission, sums up the dilemma succinctly. 'It means a choice between pig and man: man, not the pig . . . . Agricultural policy will have to be altered on a worldwide basis.'[4]

Norway is the first western country to have made this choice. Several intelligent, informed and economical measures have been taken which aim to reduce the population's meat consumption and increase the quantity of cereals and vegetables eaten. The price of grainfodder has been raised, thus making it much cheaper to raise cattle on pastures.

18

Table 2: Per capita cereal consumption[5] (in pounds)

	1964-66 average	1972-74 average	per cent increase
United States	1600	1850	16
USSR	1105	1435	30
European Community	900[1]	1000[1]	11
Japan	530[1]	620[1]	17
China	420	430	2
Developing countries (ex-China)	370[2]	395	7[2]

Source: Economic Research Service, US Department of Agriculture

[1] Figures for the cereal consumption of the European Community and to a lesser extent of Japan are reduced somewhat by the extensive use of non-cereal grains for livestock feeding. Japan's figure is also reduced by extensive direct imports of meat, which cut the livestock consumption of cereals within Japan.

[2] The 1964-66 figure was depressed in the averages by India's two bad crop years in that period. The percentage increase to 1972-74 thus exaggerates an increase that was in fact minimal.

Norway therefore achieves three things in one go: improving the health of her people; lowering the dependence on grain-fodder imports; and contributing to the reduction of the world food problem.

In the United States, where agricultural policy is above all dictated by the interests of the farmers' lobby, church groups are encouraging their members to eat less meat. Also in universities similar initiatives are gathering momentum. The argument adopted is this: if every North American and European forgoes one meal with meat in it per week, then millions of tons of grain would be released for the hungry and underfed in the Third World. The movement sees itself as a demonstration against official government policy. Similar actions with direct political leadership are under way in Britain, Switzerland, Holland and other European countries.

Of course we still have to find an answer to the question of how to finance the purchase of superfluous grain. In addition, a large proportion of this grain cannot be used for human consumption since it is of low quality and only acceptable for animal fodder. This does not weaken the argument that scanty resources such as land, fertilisers and water should be reserved solely for the production of cereals which can be directly consumed by men and not animals.

However, we must seriously consider the objection that a reduction in consumption in the rich countries does not solve the root cause of poverty itself, since it does not disturb the complex mechanism of unequal distribution and malnutrition. The excess enthusiasm which often goes with these 'relief' activities frequently diverts attention from the real problem. The reduction in consumption has only a limited significance when set against the whole host of economic, social and political measures that must be taken, not only between industrial and developing countries but within developing countries themselves.

The Shah of Iran has said that an oil price rise would 'establish a new balance between rich and poor'. The former American Treasury Secretary Mr Schulz judged the situation completely differently when he said that the developing countries were threatened with 'a terrible chain reaction of oil shortages, fertiliser shortages, food shortages and finally starvation'.

The increased price of oil, with all its related side-effects, has put heavy strains on the already limited foreign currency reserves of the non-oil-producing developing nations. In many instances, their foreign exchange in 1974 hardly covered the essential imports such as oil, fertiliser and grain, not to mention other goods necessary for development. The situation was aggravated by the simultaneous reduction of available grain through food aid programmes. The 130 non-oil-exporting developing nations are affected by the energy crisis in differing degrees, according to their economic situation.[6] They can be broken down into four main groups. To give some examples:

China, Colombia, Mexico, Bolivia and Peru are self-supporting and independent of oil imports.

Malaysia, Morocco, Zambia, Zaire and probably Brazil profit to a considerable extent from the rising prices for their exports because of the 1973/74 commodity boom, which has partially or completely balanced out the higher oil prices. However, since April 1974 commodity prices have been falling and now these countries are beginning to face more severe problems.

South Korea, Taiwan, Hong Kong and Singapore are also especially dependent on the western economic system. In addition their industries are energy-intensive. They are able however to pass on their increased production costs to their customers.

The worst hit are the forty developing countries, in tropical Africa, South Asia, Central America, the Caribbean and the Philippines, who even before the crisis were among the poorest nations of the world and had the gloomiest of prospects for the future. Their combined population totals nine hundred million — half the total population of the Third World.

Four case studies should clarify the position of those countries worst affected:[7]

INDIA: The higher oil prices raised the cost of India's import bill by 800 billion dollars in 1974, an amount which is almost two thirds of her existing reserves, over 25 per cent of her total imports and far more than the previous estimates of net capital transfer. The price rise of nitrogenous fertilisers raised the import bill by a further 500 billion dollars, and the higher price of essential grain imports added 100 billion dollars to the bill.

SRI LANKA: Despite more severe cuts in the food rations, the cost of grain imports rose by 100 million dollars in 1974. The cost of fertilisers rose by 40 million dollars and that of oil by 100 million dollars. The static world price of tea — Sri Lanka's major export commodity — has meant that the country is locked in a long-term deterioration in its terms of trade.

BANGLADESH: Bangladesh has been ravished by floods and by war and so a large proportion of her imports is for food and reconstruction. In order to realise the development programme, which must meet the needs of seventy-five million desperate people, she is forced to increase her imports. Their increased cost, which is caused by the higher oil prices, makes this impossible. Bangladesh had to pay an additional 70 million dollars for oil in 1974 and a further 100 million dollars for the increased cost of foodstuffs and fertiliser.

SAHEL COUNTRIES: Because of the devastating drought, the Sahel countries were not able to profit from the favourable world market prices for their most important export commodities — groundnuts, cotton and cattle. At the same time, since they depend on food imports, the rising cost of fuels now consumes 30 to 40 per cent of their foreign reserves — before the drought the figure was only 10 per cent. The future looks grim.

OPEC efforts to escape the lion's share of the blame for this state of affairs have been singularly unsuccessful. Much of this is their own fault. Most of their representatives regard the western press as hostile and not worth courting — no quiet briefings on airplanes from them. At the OPEC (Organisation of the Petroleum Exporting Countries) headquarters in Vienna, the vivacious Venezuelan press officer, Mrs Sabath Eljui, privately confides her bitter disappointment at the ministers' refusal to take public relations seriously. Yet there is another side to OPEC than the one presented by Dr Henry Kissinger, and gradually a picture of the oil producers' generosity is beginning to emerge — OPEC as aid-giver.

Until the great oil price rise in late 1973, only Kuwait, Libya and Saudi Arabia were providing aid on a significant scale. Estimated total net aid disbursements were about 408 million dollars in 1972 and 491 million dollars in 1973. Today, however, every OPEC country is giving and scarcely a day elapses without some announcement of a new loan or grant or concessional oil sale. Saudi Arabia, Iran, Kuwait and Venezuela are the big donors. The World Bank estimates that the total amount of aid in 1975 (as defined by the same criteria as applies to western aid, i.e. exclusive of high-interest-rate loans and military assistance) reached almost 10 billion dollars. This figure is about the same as the developing countries are paying in higher oil prices.

But OPEC aid is not quite as simple as these bald figures suggest. For although the spread of aid is increasing fast, it is still highly concentrated.

As one might expect, 60 per cent of the bilateral aid goes to Egypt, Syria and Jordan, though Pakistan, India, Sudan and Bangladesh are also major beneficiaries. But although it is true that the Islamic developing countries have done better than the other poor nations, religion has been no insuperable barrier. Most important is the fact that the amount of aid going to what the United Nations calls 'the most seriously affected countries', the poorest of the poor, is increasing. They receive nearly 40 per cent of OPEC aid, compared with only 28 per cent of western aid.

Fertiliser production is energy-intensive and therefore dependent on oil. Ninety-five per cent of nitrogenous fertiliser, which makes up about half of the total production, comes from natural gas, napthalene and by-products of petroleum. This requires vast quantities of energy and is again very dependent on oil.

The growing use of fertilisers as a result of the Green Revolution and the expansion of cultivated areas in the United States in response to the food crisis meant that before the energy crisis broke the demand for fertiliser was already beyond the capacity of existing factories.

An unofficial fertiliser embargo in the United States in 1973 plus increased buying from the world market enabled US farmers to use 9 per cent more fertilisers in 1974 than in the previous year. The same happened in Japan — Asia's main supplier of fertiliser. Meanwhile there was a shortage in the developing world of between 1.5 and 2 million tons. With that amount, 20 million tons of grain could have been produced to feed 100 million Asians or Africans for one year.

In 1974 Pakistan's imports of fertilisers met only 80 per cent of her needs. In India there was a 30 per cent shortage; Bangladesh had hardly half her total needs. Sri Lanka could only get hold of 20 to 30 per cent of her requirements. In 1975 the situation slowly began to ease. The price fell back by a third from the peak at the end of 1974. This was because of the growth in production capacity, particularly in the centrally planned economies, and the fall in demand as the reaction to the increase in price and the freight rates set in. Nevertheless the hungry countries, India, Bangladesh, Pakistan and Sri Lanka, could not import enough.[8] They just did not have the foreign exchange. The fertiliser deficit was about one million tons, according to FAO estimates. Fertilisers will remain in short supply over the next few years. For food production to keep pace with the growth in population, a 14 per cent annual increase in the use of fertilisers would be required.

Raymond Ewell, the distinguished chemical engineer, has worked out that each country needs to build one fertiliser factory for every six million inhabitants, the cost of each factory being about one hundred million dollars.[9] India's population grows annually by fifteen million people, but the

24

government is not in a position to build two and a half new factories each year. The Philippines would have to erect a factory every four years and is already eight years behind schedule on its new factory, which will only start production in two to three years' time at the earliest. On a world-wide level there should be an annual investment of eight thousand million dollars to keep pace with the growing need for fertiliser. In fact only four to five thousand million will be invested, so the gap between need and production will grow steadily.

The developing countries have become increasingly dependent on fertiliser imports from industrial countries because of the introduction of modern methods in agriculture. They have to import 49 per cent of their requirements, producing 51 per cent themselves; even so, in many cases the raw materials for fertiliser manufacture are still imported. And we must realise that these figures merely signify what can be afforded and do not equate with the real, effective needs.

The industrialised countries use 85 per cent of fertilisers, yet they have only 30 per cent of the world's population. It is estimated that the per capita consumption of fertilisers in the industrialised countries is 110 pounds; in the developing countries it is a mere 12 pounds. The differences are even more extreme when one looks at the use per hectare. In Western Europe in 1972, 146 pounds of nitrogenous fertilisers were used per hectare, in North America about 66 pounds per hectare. In Latin America the figure was 25 pounds, in the Middle East 21 pounds and in the Far East 22 pounds.

An additional fertiliser input produces much greater outputs from countries with low fertiliser consumption than the same addition would produce in Western Europe and America, where the soil is approaching saturation-point. One additional ton of fertiliser produces five extra tons of grain in Europe, Japan or the USA. In India, Brazil or Indonesia an extra ton would increase productivity by eight to ten tons. From a global perspective, for the industrialised countries to reduce the quantities available to the developing countries when supplies are scarce is an irresponsible short-term measure. It is even more absurd when one realises that, for

Table 3: The cost of scarcity: import of manufactured fertilisers by developing countries (Source: IMF)

		1971	*1972*[1]	*1973*[1]	*1974*[1]
Nitrogen	million tons	2.3	2.5	2.6	2.0
	million US$	311	341	462	900
Phosphate	million tons	1.0	1.2	1.4	1.1
	million US$	126	183	275	380
Potash	million tons	1.3	1.5	1.8	1.8
	million US$	96	101	138	170

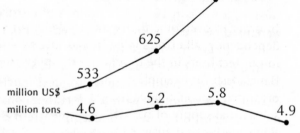

Total

[1] Estimates.

every pound sterling that the developing countries are unable to spend on fertiliser this year, they will have to spend five pounds on grain imports next year.

Few of us ever think of the quantities of fertiliser that are strewn over lawns, parks and golf courses in the rich countries. In the United States alone this amounts to three million tons a year — more than the total deficit felt by the poor countries in 1974. In Britain only 100,000 tons of fertiliser, out of our total consumption of five million tons, are used for food production. Instead of feeding green and healthy lawns in the United States and Britain, this same amount of fertiliser could have helped to produce enough grain for 150 million people.

These calculations are of course theoretical and contestable, but they illustrate that the current food crisis could be overcome with an improved mechanism of distribution, regulated by those who need most, not by those who can afford most. The shortage has increased the dependence of the Third World countries on the industrialised countries for vitally needed fertilisers. During the hearings of the United States Senate Committee on Agriculture in the summer of 1974, it was reported that in that year no less than two thirds of the fertiliser set aside by the USA for overseas aid went to South Vietnam. The rest had to be divided between Pakistan, Bangladesh, Kenya, Guatemala and Honduras.[10]

In order to overcome the two crucial elements of shortage and dependency, all efforts must be put into raising the production of fertilisers in the developing countries themselves. Bangladesh for example could soon, if she would get herself organised, become independent of imports, thanks to her substantial supply of natural gas. This could prove to be Bangladesh's best answer to the problem of feeding her hungry millions.[11]

It is plain that during the present bottleneck the choice for developing countries is 'fertilisers or famine'. Yet although this problem is so urgent, we should not conclude without a word of caution: we are not advocating the development of agriculture in the Third World along the lines of the North American model, namely through mechanisation and high

27

consumption of fertilisers and pesticides. An analysis by John and Carol Steinhart of Wisconsin University concludes that if all countries produced their food by the methods of US farmers, 80 per cent of the world's existing energy supplies would be required for the production of food alone.[12] Five to ten calories of energy are required to produce one calorie of food in industrialised societies. In contrast, farmers in developing countries can produce five to ten calories of food with only one calorie of energy.

So we must devise an 'Alternative Agriculture', improving outputs per hectare with fewer energy inputs. Instead of obtaining fertilisers from the atmosphere by energy-intensive means, the potential to fix nitrogen through plants must be developed. Biologically correct rotation of crops can radically reduce the need for artificial fertilisers. Careful utilisation of organic fertilisers and waste products is a further answer to the problem of reducing dependency on expensive and scarce energy. Finally the correct balance between animal husbandry and arable farming must be found, one which provides biological equilibrium and at the same time makes the small farmer independent of expensive inputs and exploitative credit systems. Alternative Agriculture does not imply a step backwards to extensive cultivation but rather a movement to a new form of farming based on biological and ecological principles.[13]

The theory that the race against hunger can only be overcome by introducing modern agricultural technology is refuted by the example of China. Since the 1949 Revolution, China has escaped from chronic famine through intensive farming along the traditional lines, rather than by using intensive forms of energy. She has done this despite a doubling of population between 1949 and today and with the smallest per capita land-holdings in the world. The basis of this achievement is not a new technology but social revolution.[14]

Optimism and pessimism over the world food situation fluctuate with the weather. The outlook was gloomy in 1965 and 1966 when bad weather caused cereal production in the developing nations to fall behind population growth. But during the elated mood caused by the success of the Green Revolution, people quickly forgot that favourable weather was an essential factor for success and, unfortunately, one that was impossible to influence. Then in 1971 bad weather ended the euphoria. In 1972 the situation worsened. In the Ukraine the weather was too cold for the winter wheat, in India the monsoon was too late, in the Sahel the drought intensified, insufficient rain fell in Argentina and Australia, while abnormally damp weather reduced the maize and soya harvest in the United States. For the first time since the Second World War, world food production fell in absolute figures, and in the developing nations per capita production fell 3 per cent below the average production for 1961-65. 1973 was a good year. But then in 1974 there was bad weather again. For only the second time in thirty years the world crop fell.

The development of irrigation, drainage and water reservoirs, the cultivation of quick-ripening varieties, mechanisation and improved storing techniques have all made it possible to reduce the dependency of agriculture on the weather. But in spite of all this, cereal production over large areas is still exposed to the variables of uncertain climate, with consequences such as the fourteen tons' fall in production in the Soviet Union in 1972 and the forty million tons' increase in the following year. Only a third of the agricultural land in Russia lies south of the 49th parallel which is the area most suited to cereals and only 1.1 per cent of this land receives more than an average of twenty-eight inches of rainfall a year.

Although rainfall and other climatic factors have the most influence on harvest, one should not underestimate the impact of such factors as fluctuations in employment, changes in income and prices, changes in agricultural policy, and the onset of war and natural catastrophes. Often these changes cancel others out and a rough balance results worldwide. Only approximate figures are available for fluctuations in production of individual countries and continents. If we take the average production over several years, yields in any given year range from 4 per cent above to 4 per cent below the mean. Thus the fall in production as a result of bad weather in 1972 was no extreme occurrence but lies within the bounds of normal expectations.

Walter Orr Roberts, a leading climatologist at the National Centre for Climatic Research, Boulder, Colorado, believes we are at the beginning of a period in which the world climate will deteriorate. The unproductive harvest in 1972 was only the beginning of a long series. If his prognosis is correct then this adverse climate will become the norm, as in the cold period between 1880 and 1920. The participants in an international workshop in Bonn in May 1974 came to a similar conclusion. They expected a cooler climatic period which would balance the former changeable weather, the drought and heatwaves. Even the optimistic amongst them could in no way escape the conclusion that the international politics of grain production would be determined by extended poor harvests in the next ten years.[15]

According to a Central Intelligence Agency report, 'Political Implications of Trends in World Population, Food Production and Climate', all countries in the high latitudes, particularly the northern regions of Canada, China and the Soviet Union and equatorial regions dependent on the monsoon, would be affected by the deteriorating climate. Countries in the mid-latitudes would be least affected. The obvious conclusion of this argument is the further intensification of the world's dependence on the breadbasket of the United States (see chapter 11).

Such dependence is not new. Until the Second World War Latin America, North America, Eastern Europe and Australia were the most important grain exporters. Since then North America has become the world's dominant grain supplier.

In addition North America is the major exporter of rice and soya (90 per cent of the world market). The United States and Canada have similar weather cycles and they cannot be expected never to have a bad harvest. Research has shown convincingly that North America suffers from periods of drought at twenty-year intervals, and these cycles can be traced back to the time of the Civil War. Since the last dry period was observed at the beginning of the 1950s the next

dry spell must be imminent. Indeed it is possible that it
began in the summer of 1974. It is true that improved
techniques preventing soil erosion, together with irrigation
installations, will minimise damage and avoid a repetition of
the dustbowls of the 1930s. But with almost exhausted
reserves, growing demand and the dependence of the whole
world on this one granary, it needs a drop in production of
only a few per cent to create a very dangerous situation.
From these facts one can draw the conclusion that, just as
the world financial system can no longer count on the dollar
as its base, North American agriculture is no longer a guarantee
for the security of world nutrition.

This degree of dependence is frightening, not only because
it concerns the security of many millions of people, but above
all because of its implications for power politics. The United
States with its large proportion of the world's grain supply has
the power to decide the fate of the hungry masses in the
world. The CIA report already mentioned argues that this
'could give the United States a measure of power it had never
had before — possibly an economic and political dominance
greater than that of the immediate post-World War II years'.
In political terms the same policy can be undertaken with

Table 4: *The changing pattern of world grain trade (millions
of metric tons)*[16]

Region	1934-38	1972[1]
North America	+5	+84
Latin America	+9	−4
Western Europe	−24	−21
Eastern Europe + USSR	+5	−27
Africa	+1	−5
Asia	+2	−35
Australia and New Zealand	+3	+8

[1] Preliminary figures.

grain which the oil-exporting Arab states practised during the Yom Kippur war with oil. The Secretary of State, Henry Kissinger, and the Secretary for Agriculture, Earl Butz, have not tried to hide the fact that the United States is ready to play off the 'food weapon' against the 'oil weapon'. Her proportion of the world grain market is bigger than the Arabs' share of the energy market.

The conclusions are obvious. All efforts should be made to increase the production capacity of the other continents, so that the world is not dependent on the climate and political discretion of the United States.

Many people see the explosive population growth rate in the Third World as the fundamental cause of the food crisis. If this be the case, they say, then it is crucial to encourage radical birth control campaigns. The relevance of this approach will be critically analysed in this chapter.

In the first fifteen centuries of the Christian era the population grew between 2 and 5 per cent per century. Today in a whole string of developing countries the *yearly* population growth rate is more than 3 per cent. African countries with growth rates of over 3 per cent include Algeria, Kenya, Liberia, Libya, Morocco, Rhodesia, Sudan and Tunisia. In Latin America, Costa Rica, the Dominican Republic, El Salvador, Honduras, Mexico, Columbia, Equador, Paraguay, Peru, Surinam and Venezuela fall into this category; in Asia Iraq, Jordan, Kuwait, East Malaysia, Mongolia, Pakistan, Philippines, Syria, Thailand and Fiji. The consequences of this exponential growth rate are almost unimaginable, because such rates soon take on astronomical proportions.

The Club of Rome study *The Limits to Growth*[17] made vivid use of the parable of the water-lily pond in portraying the effect of exponential population growth in a finite planet. A water-lily is growing in a pond. It doubles itself each day, so that on the second day there are two leaves, on the third day four, and so on. On the twenty-ninth day the pond is *half* full. But on the thirtieth day the *whole* surface of the water is covered with the water lily.

A population growth of 1 per cent per year means an

increase of over two and a half times (270 per cent) per
century. With a growth rate of 2 per cent per year the
population increases seven times over one hundred years. The
populations of those developing nations with growths of over
3 per cent will increase about twenty to thirty fold within a
century. In Mexico alone there could be a population of 1.3
thousand million by the year 2070. In those developing
countries which have growth rates between 2.4 and 3.8 per
cent, the population will double before the end of the
century. They have the highest growth rates in man's history.

Another way of picturing the almost unimaginable dynam-
ism of population growth is to look at the time intervals during

Table 5[18]

Percentage increase of population per year	Percentage increase in population per century
1	270 per cent or more than double
2	700 per cent or seven times
4	1900 per cent or nineteen times
5	5100 per cent or fifty-one times

Table 6[19]

	Number of years to reach the next thousand million	Reached in the year
First thousand million	2,000,000	1830
Second thousand million	100	1930
Third thousand million	30	1960
Fourth thousand million	15	1975
Fifth thousand million	11	1986
Sixth thousand million	9	1995

33

which it took, or will take, for another thousand million people to be added to the world population.

The projections of the United Nations Organisation, on which table 6 is based, anticipate a slowing down of the growth rate in later stages. They work on the assumption that growth rates in all regions will eventually fall to 'replacement level', i.e. to the level where the population no longer increases (2.1 children per couple). All the projections are based on a number of arbitrary assumptions and should be reviewed constantly.

The United Nations have in fact drawn up three variants. Even the lowest and most optimistic reckons that the world population will be stabilised only at the end of the twenty-first century, at just below the 10 thousand million level. The middle variant, which has been described by the UN demographers as 'relatively optimistic', puts stabilisation of the population figures in the year 2125, with 12.3 thousand million people. (It is on this middle variant that the FAO bases its assessments.) The 'highest' variant — and at the same time the gloomiest one — forecasts stability only in the year 2135 with a total population of 16 thousand million.[20] The differences result from the varying assessment of that point in time at which individual nations will reach 'replacement fertility'.

The middle variant assumes that all regions will reach this point between 2010 and 2065, the industrialised countries first and developing nations later. (For the factors which lead to a reduction in the growth rates see chapter 10.) The greater part of the increase of course will be registered in the developing nations: the lowest variant reckons with a population of 7.9 thousand million in the developing regions and the highest one with 14.1 thousand million in these areas. These projections should in no way be misinterpreted as prophecies, for they are of an essentially demographic nature and completely ignore important factors, such as ecological problems, energy needs, situations of social and political stress, that must arise from this colossal pressure of population. In the final analysis, if the earth can't support its population, people die.

34

This question of the ultimate limits of the earth's carrying ability is too often overlooked. So many projections which blithely stretch into the future neglect to face this simple reality of life.

In pre-industrial society death rates were extremely high as a result of high infant and child mortality and the generally low life expectancy. To ensure family continuity parents had large families. During the eighteenth century with the onset of sewerage, improved health care and hygiene, the death rates in Europe, which had been at between twenty-eight and thirty-two per thousand, sank by about ten points, while birth rates remained at the same level. Population growth began to spurt ahead — the rates of increase doubled from 0.5 to 1 per cent. It was only towards the middle of the nineteenth century that birth rates began to fall.

From this development was deduced the theory of 'Demographic Transition' which argues that the population explosion at the beginning of the modernisation process is automatically followed by a fall in the birth rate and a normalisation of the relationship between birth and death rates as a result of the increasing improvement in the standard of living.

Whether this theory is true or not is a burning topic, for since the Second World War all developing nations have recorded rapidly falling death rates. They are almost without exception in the first phase of Demographic Transition. This fall was brought about by medical technology, which made it possible to eliminate or to cure at a low cost, primarily by vaccinations, a host of killer diseases.

But the demographic process in developing nations is nevertheless taking a different course from the one it took in the 'model case' of Europe. And this is leading to far greater pressures than existed in the corresponding phases in Europe and North America. Thus, with a rate of increase of 2.5 per cent, the population of the developing countries doubles every twenty-eight years, while in developing Europe with a rate of 1 per cent it took seventy years for the population to double. The higher rates of increase in the developing countries are caused by the much swifter fall in the death rates. The same process in Europe and North America was spread over a whole century.

In addition, many developing nations lack areas where it is easy to settle new population. Europe used the Americas, Africa and Australasia. In 1900 only 44 per cent of the population of the United States and Canada was under twenty years old. In developing nations this age group, which is unproductive from the economic point of view, usually makes up 50 to 60 per cent of the population.

In the short term it is scarcely possible to correct the self-perpetuation of demographic trends. For Gunnar Myrdal the distinguished development economist, the most important feature of this population growth is that 'within the next decades, government action, no matter how vigorous, determined and concentrated, could do very little, if anything, to hold in check the powerful social forces propelling it. Even if fertility were to decline substantially during the next decades . . . this would not change the trend in population size very much within the span of three decades after decline began.'[21] Even a drop in fertility below the 'replacement level' could not prevent the population from continuing to expand for the next seventy years. Only then would an actual decline in population take place. To slow down the population growth and above all the increase in the population of employable age will take an extraordinarily long braking distance.

The questions Whether demographic rates can be influenced, What factors lead to a fall in the birth rate, and When will this fall begin? have become fateful issues for Mankind. A United Nations study made in the early 1960s, which tried to relate fertility and various indices of social and economic well-being, came to the following conclusion. 'In a developing country where fertility is initially high, improving economic and social conditions is likely to have little if any effect on fertility until a certain economic and social level is reached; but once that level is achieved, fertility is likely to enter a decided decline and to continue downward until it is again stabilized on a much lower plane.'[22]

In general there seems to be a connection between falling birth rates and the level of education and job opportunities for women. But it has proved impossible to establish with quantitative details a socio-economic threshold where the fall in the birth rate begins. In the United States the fall in birth rate figures only began when the average income had reached a relatively high level, while in Korea, Sri Lanka and Taiwan the fall started when per capita income was still below two hundred dollars. China started the process with an even lower level of average income.

Nevertheless there is one common factor. In nearly all countries with falling birth figures the process was initiated when the majority of the population began to receive a share of a combination of social and economic improvements. According to Rich,[23] who is an advocate of this theory, this factor is true for a broad spectrum of countries with such varying conditions as Taiwan, China, South Korea, Singapore, Hong Kong, Uruguay, Costa Rica and Sri Lanka.

Conversely, in countries with relatively high economic growth where the benefits of this growth are not however brought to a wide section of the population, the birth rates remain high, as for example in Venezuela and Mexico. The decisive factor is not the level of gross national product but the equality of income distribution. This theory is not undisputed and has to be confirmed by further studies.

However there is enough evidence to suggest that family planning campaigns will only be successful where parents have some share in broad social and economic improvements and through this are motivated towards planned contraception. The decision to have a small family will only become possible once care in old age is guaranteed other than by having a large number of children. Infant mortality must reach a low enough level for every child born to have a high chance of survival. It thus becomes clear why so many governments which have undertaken a population control programme have yet so far hardly influenced the rate of growth — even though 87 per cent of the population of the Third World are ruled by such governments.

37

With these arguments as background the common belief that better medical care accelerates population growth must be put into a new perspective. If better medical care is part of a better social system, within which broad sections of the community have access to better education, to employment and incomes, to better agricultural techniques (and thereby receive more adequate nutrition), then medicine too can become an important factor in the strategy to check population growth.

In the view of Walter H. Pawley, former director of the FAO planning staff and of the IWP (Indicative World Plan for Agricultural Development) it is quite possible to guarantee the feeding of thirty-six billion people within one hundred years. Two pre-conditions have to be fulfilled: the development of techniques that will enable a permanent use of land in the tropic zones after the land has been cleared of tropical forest, and the rational de-salination of sea-water.

Such long-term optimism where ecological problems are shunted to one side stands in marked contrast to the far more pessimistic outlook for the immediate future. *Can food production keep up with population growth today and tomorrow?* And how can the urgently needed improvement in the quality of nutrition be achieved at the same time? Reference-points for judging the present situation and development in the next decade up to 1985 are available from the trends of the last decades.

Since the Second World War average annual world production has regularly increased at a greater pace than population growth. But apart from Africa and North America rates of increase in all continents were slowing down as the 1960s ended. Between 1971 and 1973 60 per cent of world production was in the hands of the industrialised countries, who numbered 30 per cent of the world's population. Accordingly they played the principal role in supply.

Before the Second World War the developing countries were in general net exporters of cereals, but under the pressure of the population explosion they have increasingly become importers, although, in spite of all the economic

38

difficulties they were able to increase their agricultural production during the 1950s and 1960s by the same amount that production was increased in industrialised countries. This achievement is unique. But for all that the rising rates of production in many developing nations just could not keep pace with population growth.

Table 7 compares the trends in food production with the growth in population of seventy-one developing countries. In twenty-four countries, one third of the list, production between 1953 and 1971 fell behind population growth. Moreover if one takes into account the influence of the rise in incomes in thirty-nine of the seventy-one countries (with 63 per cent of the population of the seventy-one nations) production could not meet demand.

The number of countries with a negative trend seems to have increased in the last few years. Between 1961 and 1971 population grew faster than food production in forty-two out of ninety-two developing nations. What is worse, countries which for ten to fifteen years were obtaining rates of increase of 5 or more per cent are now recording drops. This indication of a slackening development makes all projections based on the easily achieved successes of the last decade at least questionable.

When one begins to look at the plans for future increases in production, one must record the pessimistic fact that the targets of forty-seven national development plans were only reached in seventeen cases. Also the annual production increase of 4 per cent as provided for in the international strategy for the UN's Second Development Decade, 1960-1970, has not been achieved in any region. Only one third (twenty-one) of sixty-two countries have reached the target which the FAO's World Indicative Plan (WIP) set for 1961/63-1975 (with far lower rates than those set for each of the national development plans). Instead of the 3.4 per cent rise set by the WIP the developing nations reached on average a rise of 2.9 per cent. If the target for the Second Development Decade is still to be reached then an annual increase of 5 per cent will be necessary for the remaining years of the decade.

Interestingly the unsuccessful attempt to increase food production in proportion to population increase and growing demand does not coincide either with especially high or with especially low birth rates in individual countries. Out of twenty-five countries with growth rates of 3 or more per cent per year, ten did not keep production up with the population increase, four managed to keep pace, and in eleven nations demand was met or surpassed even with the growth in demand because of higher incomes. In the view of the FAO the deciding factor is not the increase in population alone but also the capability of governments to carry out a suitable agricultural policy. The FAO feels the causes for the non-fulfilment of the agricultural development plans lie in the following areas:

1 The productivity of the cultivated areas has lagged (although the cultivated land surface has increased quicker than was foreseen). This can be put down to a delay in the expansion of irrigation systems and insufficient exploitation of available capacity.

2 The introduction of the new high-yielding varieties of rice seems to be running into more technical difficulties than had been foreseen.

3 Until recently the use of fertilisers was going according to plan but a sharp fall has been recorded as a result of the oil crisis (see chapter 2).

4 The number of tractors has increased faster than expected but has caused more unemployment.

5 The government agricultural organisation and departments have been used too often as mere services and not enough as a means to mobilise the farmers.

6 Agrarian reform is still lacking in most countries or gives no benefit to the small farmer.

7 The credit systems favour the big farmer, and attempts at self-help in cooperatives or similar groups are still insufficient.

Shortly after the First World War Walter Mallory, who had worked in the International Commission on food aid to China, wrote in his well-documented book, *China, Land of*

Table 7: Trends in food production in 71 developing countries[1] in relation to population growth and domestic demand

	Average annual rate of growth[2]				Net cereal imports as percentage of domestic supply	Population mid-1972
	Food production[3]	Population	Per caput income[4]	Estimated domestic demand[5] for food		
	1953-71		1955-70		1966-70	1972
	...........per cent per year...........				per cent	millions
	(1)	(2)	(3)	(4)	(5)	(6)
1 Production failed to equal population growth						
Algeria	−0.1	2.4	1.5	3.4	25.4	14.5
Zaire	0.1	2.3	0.4	2.6	24.6	18.3
Uruguay	0.8	1.3	−0.8	1.2	−	2.9
Chad	0.9	1.5	−1.5	0.6	1.1	3.7
Haiti	1.0	1.9	−0.1	1.8	6.5	5.0
Tunisia	1.1	1.8	2.0	3.2	42.0	5.5
Mauritius	1.3	2.6	0.8	3.0	99.2	0.9
Dahomey	1.5	2.9	−3.5	0.7	5.6	2.9
Jamaica	1.5	1.9	3.0	3.3	97.9	2.0
Jordan	1.8	3.1	5.4	6.5	51.3	2.4
Uganda	1.8	2.5	1.6	3.3	2.8	9.0
Trinidad and Tobago	1.9	2.6	4.6	4.9	93.1	1.0
Nigeria	2.0	3.0	1.6	3.7	2.3	71.9
Syrian Arab Republic	2.0	2.9	2.9	4.5	14.7	6.6
Chile	2.1	2.5	1.8	3.3	20.8	10.2
El Salvador	2.1	3.0	1.9	4.1	16.0	3.7
Indonesia	2.1	2.4	0.1	2.5	4.3	126.0
Dominican Republic	2.2	3.6	0.6	3.9	30.9	4.6
Guyana	2.5	3.1	1.1	3.7	− [6]	0.8
Kenya	2.6	3.0	2.9	4.7	− [6]	11.4
Paraguay	2.6	2.8	1.0	3.1	21.6	2.5
Iraq	2.8	3.3	2.9	5.2	1.7	10.4
Saudi Arabia	2.9	3.1	5.5	5.7	64.2	5.7
Philippines	3.2	3.3	1.7	4.3	9.0	41.2

Source: Preliminary assessment of the World Food Situation, World Food Conference 1974, UNIE/Conf.65/Prep./6 April 1974, p.33

Table 7 (continued)

	(1)	*(2)*	*(3)*	*(4)*	*(5)*	*(6)*

2 **Production equalled or exceeded population growth**

A Production growth failed to equal growth of domestic demand

Argentina	1.8	1.7	1.9	2.0	$-^7$	25.0
Ethiopia	2.3	1.9	2.1	3.1	0.6	26.4
Burma	2.4	2.0	2.6	3.1	$-^7$	28.8
India	2.4	2.3	1.6	3.2	6.2	578.0
Mauritania	2.4	1.8	4.1	2.8	29.9	1.2
Sierra Leone	2.4	1.3	4.2	3.2	12.2	2.6
Mozambique	2.7	1.4	2.8	2.9	6.0	7.7
Morocco	3.0	2.9	0.6	3.2	10.0	16.5
Pakistan[8]	3.0	2.9	1.8	4.1	3.4	139.3
Peru	3.0	2.9	1.7	3.9	31.4	14.4
Colombia	3.2	3.2	1.4	3.8	12.2	22.5
Turkey	3.2	2.6	2.7	3.7	1.9	37.0
Iran	3.3	2.9	6.1	6.5	2.3	30.2
Khmer Republic	3.5	2.7	2.1	4.2	$-^7$	7.6
Zambia	4.3	3.0	3.9	4.9	1.9	4.6
Korea, Republic of	4.4	2.8	4.7	4.8	16.0	14.4
Panama	4.4	3.2	3.9	4.8	16.4	1.6

B Production growth equalled or exceeded growth of domestic demand

Angola	2.7	1.4	2.2	2.6	–	5.6
Central African Republic	2.8	1.9	−1.7	1.2	10.9	2.2
Madagascar	2.8	2.4	−0.5	2.1	$-^7$	7.1
Tanzania	3.2	2.5	1.1	3.1	2.4	14.0
Cameroon	3.3	2.0	1.7	2.7	7.4	6.0
Senegal	3.3	2.2	−2.2	1.2	26.4	4.0
Gabon	3.6	0.9	4.8	2.7	84.6	0.5
Sri Lanka	3.6	2.4	1.6	3.0	43.2	13.0
Egypt	3.7	2.5	2.3	3.7	18.1	35.1
Ghana	3.9	2.7	0.8	3.0	17.6	9.3
Rhodesia	3.9	3.2	1.4	3.9	$-^7$	5.6

Table 7 (continued)

	(1)	(2)	(3)	(4)	(5)	(6)
Brazil	4.1	3.0	3.0	4.0	6.5	99.3
Niger	4.1	2.6	−1.4	2.0	−[7]	4.2
Guatemala	4.2	2.9	2.3	4.1	9.9	5.5
Honduras	4.2	3.3	1.7	4.2	2.2	2.8
Sudan	4.3	2.9	1.7	3.9	8.0	16.5
Malawi	4.7	2.6	2.5	3.8	−[7]	4.8
Bolivia	4.8	2.5	0.8	2.9	28.7	5.2
Upper Volta	4.8	1.8	−1.4	1.2	2.1	5.5
Ivory Coast	4.9	3.3	1.0	3.7	20.2	5.2
Mexico	4.9	3.4	2.8	4.3	−[7]	54.3
Malaysia, West	5.1	3.0	2.1	4.1	34.6	9.9
Nicaragua	5.1	3.0	2.1	3.9	12.0	2.2
Ecuador	5.2	3.3	1.2	4.0	11.4	6.5
Thailand	5.3	3.1	3.2	4.6	−[7]	38.0
Togo	5.4	2.4	0.3	2.5	4.3	1.9
Costa Rica	5.7	3.8	2.7	4.8	33.8	1.9
Cyprus	5.8	1.3	3.8	2.5	38.1	0.6
Lebanon	5.8	3.0	0.7	3.3	86.8	2.8
Venezuela	6.0	3.7	1.5	4.2	46.0	11.8

[1] Countries in each group listed in ascending order of production increase.

[2] Compound interest.

[3] Food component of crop and livestock production, excluding fish production; trend rate of growth, compound interest.

[4] Real GDP per caput.

[5] Calculated on basis of growth of population and per caput income in columns 2 and 3 and estimates of income elasticity of farm-gate demand for food in Agricultural Commodity Projections 1970-80 FAO, Rome, 1971.

[6] Net exporter.

[7] Net exporter.

[8] Including Bangladesh.

Famine, 'And now a final word on the population problem. In my view overpopulation is the most important factor in the latest Chinese famine.'[24] At that time the population of China was less than three hundred million; in 1973 it was approaching eight hundred million. Since the Revolution in 1949 the population of China has doubled, but over the same period China has overcome the age-old problem of hunger. It has achieved this with the smallest cultivable plots of land per person in the whole world.[25]

The whole notion of 'overpopulation' has turned out to be very debatable. There is hardly any satisfactory definition of this term, which has so many connotations. It is not numerical ratios which are crucial for the solution of the world food problem, but rather the social and economic factors which determine the *production* and the *distribution* of the end product.

At the World Population Conference held in Bucharest in August 1974, nearly all the developing countries united to support this theme. They were suspicious that since the industrialised countries were leading the birth control campaigns, they would play down any line of attack bar the contraceptive one. The industrialised countries try to get round the question of how far their economic domination of the Third World intensifies inequality, how far they are therefore an additional cause of the problems of population and hunger. The industrialised countries would do well to take note of these opinions.

As the grain elevators are emptied and the grain shortage on
the world market sets off high prices, people begin to talk of
a world food crisis. But suffering and famine exist despite
periods of bad weather and despite the oil crisis.

We all think we understand the realities of hunger. Reports
of famine in the Sahel, Ethiopia, Bangladesh and India have
put us in the picture. Children with extended stomachs, old
shrivelled faces and people dying of starvation on the streets.
But hunger is not limited to those emaciated people, who are
the first to die in a famine. They are only the tip of the ice
berg. 'The lack of any of these constituents of a balanced diet
causes premature death, though not necessarily from
emaciation due to lack of any kind of food that can be eaten.
Lack of any kind of food, as occurs in famine, has always
been a major cause of death. In the last decade more people
died from famine than were killed in war. But these numbers
are small when compared with the number whose diet is
inadequate to maintain health.' So wrote Lord Boyd Orr, the
first Secretary-General of the FAO, in 1952 in the foreword
to the second edition of *The Geography of Hunger* by Jose
de Castro. This kind of hidden hunger captures much less
sympathy than spectacular famine, but its social costs are far
greater.

Our reflections on the subject so far have shown us that
the mechanisms of global production and distribution produce
deficits for some and a surplus for others. But we have to go
way beyond this self-evident conclusion if we are to compre-
hend fully the realities of hunger.

First we must define the terms undernourishment and
malnutrition. The term undernourishment implies a quanti-
tive lack of calories. This calorie requirement depends on age,
sex, size, body weight, average yearly temperature and above

all the amount of physical work. The average need for an adult is about 2,700 calories per day.

As well as these energy requirements, the body also needs protein for body-building. The quality of diet not only depends on a protein source but is affected by types of amino acids in vegetable and animal protein. Protein from animals is better than that from vegetables. The protein requirements are 0.57 grammes per kilo of body weight for an adult. The requirements are greater for children since they need more body-building materials for normal growth. The result of protein deficiency is malnutrition.

There is a delicate balance between protein and calorie needs. If the calorie requirements cannot be met by the diet, then the body uses a proportion of the available protein as an energy source. The protein is then not used in its body-building function. In developing countries many people, particularly children, are malnourished, despite the theoretical adequacy of their protein intake. In effect it is the calorie intake which is used as a measure of the sufficiency or inadequacy of diets. The lack of vitamins and minerals as well as protein is an important factor in malnutrition.

Very careful estimates based on calorie requirements showed that in the early 1960s in normal harvest conditions four hundred million people were insufficiently fed (see table 8). Jose de Castro, from other reliable estimates, puts the total much higher: two thirds of the world's population suffers from hunger and two billion people cannot find the wherewithal to fight hunger.

If we take average estimates, one in every eight people suffered from hunger in 1970. Nineteen out of every twenty hungry people live in developing countries. In South-East Asia, where there is the highest concentration of underfed people, three in every ten people go hungry. In Africa this ratio is one person in four. In the Near East it is one in five. And in Latin America every eighth person is malnourished.[1]

Worst off are the children. Some ten million children are directly threatened with death. Eighty million suffer from quite dangerous malnutrition and a further 120 million suffer from light malnutrition. In total, it seems that a half to two thirds of the world's small children are inadequately fed.

Genuine regions of starvation at present include Angola, Somalia and the Sahel countries in the continent of Africa: Afghanistan, Saudi Arabia and both Yemens in the Middle East; Bolivia, El Salvador and Haiti in Latin America; India, Bangladesh and Sri Lanka in Asia. The UN has a list of thirty-three countries which it considers the most seriously affected.

The question 'What is the total food shortage for all mal-fed people?' can only be answered with estimates. A small additional ration of 250 calories per person per day would require twelve million tons more cereal each year. In comparison with the 373 million tons which the industrialised countries use as animal feed grains, the twelve-million-ton deficit would in theory seem easy to overcome. Another comparison is just as plausible: in 1974 the amount of

Table 8: Estimated number of people with insufficient protein/energy supply by regions (1970)

Region	Population	Percentage below lower limit	Number below lower limit
	(thousand million)	(per cent)	(millions)
Developed regions	1.07	3	28
Developing regions excluding Asian centrally-planned economies	1.75	20	360
Latin America	0.28	13	37
Far East	1.02	22	221
Near East	0.17	20	34
Africa	0.28	25	68
World (excluding Asian centrally-planned economies)	2.83	14	388

47

dehydrated milk and milk powders fed to cattle was three times as great as the amount imported by developing countries. About half this amount would have been sufficient to give two hundred million undernourished children a daily ration of 100 grammes of milk.[2] It is faulty distribution systems and not inadequate production which cause starvation! But before we examine the distribution mechanism, we must look into the consequences of starvation.

The unequal distribution of food is evident between continents, between countries, between social groups and even at the family level. Household studies have shown that working adults keep the largest share of available food for themselves. For pregnant and breast-feeding women and for children, who are especially in need of protein-rich food, there are often only the inadequate left-overs.

Badly fed children have their physical growth retarded and their mental development is often irreparably damaged during the most important phase of brain development, the first four years of life. The worst forms of protein-calorie deficiency are *kwashiorkor* and *marasmus*. In poor states these diseases are found in 0.5 to 5 per cent of all children between one and five. As a result of *kwashiorkor* alone millions of children in the Third World die before they are five.[3]

In addition there is a large number of children who are not directly affected by diseases related to malnutrition but who also die from other diseases like tuberculosis, whooping cough or infection of the bowels because their undernourished bodies cannot provide any resistance. Once they are infected their ability to take in and make use of food drops. Through this the child becomes rapidly weaker and even more liable to illness.

In 1974 in Brazil it was largely the underfed and malnourished children who fell victims of meningitis. Research by the World Health Organisation (WHO) has found that 69 per cent of the 600,000 children who die every year in Brazil were victims of diseases which caused more fatalities than usual because of the inadequate diets available. In many developing countries 30 to 40 per cent of all deaths are accounted for by children under five years old. Eighteen to thirty in every thousand two-year-old children die. The equivalent figures for well-fed children in industrialised countries are 7 per cent and less than ten in every thousand.

The social effects are disastrous, since, in order to be sure of children living over the critical age of about five, each family has to have a high number of children in the first place. In many developing countries the gap between births is very close to the biological minimum. This narrow gap is another cause of a specific illness in small children. The children are weaned too early as the mother quickly becomes pregnant again. In Bulacan, a province north of Manila in the Philippines, research has shown that in families that produced a new child every eighteen months 55 per cent of the children were weaned too early and consequently suffered from malnutrition. On the other hand, in families where the time between births was thirty-one months, the proportion of undernourished children fell to 28.5 per cent. In Africa the expression *'kwashiorkor'* (pushed from the mother's breast) was coined for the illness caused by lack of protein.

Studies show that the size of the family affects the amount of food available for children. The worst forms of protein-calorie deficiency are found in families with more than four children. The vicious circle of hunger and overpopulation is apparent: hunger creates higher mortality in children and this means that larger families are needed. Thus these children are poorly fed and have a low chance of living — as de Castro wrote 'it is not overpopulation that causes hunger, but rather hunger causes overpopulation.'

For a large proportion of the population hunger is a life-long experience. Chronic hunger induces depression and apathy. 'Those who are affected by it quickly lose their appetite, their motivations and their energy for work', argues Castro. He even goes as far as to suggest that 'Chinese conformism', 'the fate of India's lowest caste' and 'the carelessness of many people in Latin America' can be explained by the deficiency of particular amino acids present in egg whites in all these people's diets.

In its analysis of the *World Food Crisis* the Society of German Scientists stated that: 'The lethargy and shyness for hard work which is sometimes to be observed in the tropics cannot be traced back to the climate or lack of will to work. It is a self-preserving check that is caused by insufficient nutrition. These people are consequently less capable of performing as a work force, are liable to have accidents at work and are threatened by illness.'[4] The result for both individuals and the collective societies of the developing countries is a vicious circle of undernourishment, inadequate work performance and growing poverty.

However insufficient the statistics may be, one thing is clear; since 1970 the number of people starving has rapidly increased. Alongside the Sahel and in the Indian subcontinent, where famine resulted from drought and floods respectively, are other areas which suffer because of poor economic conditions, rising costs of living and growing unemployment. This kind of creeping famine is very difficult to control. The cost of food gives us an indication.

In Bangladesh, the price of grains doubled between January and August 1974. In the space of four years the price has risen at least fivefold whereas wages have risen only very slightly. An average family had to spend 11 *Taka* on its daily rice requirements in the autumn of 1974, yet the available income for an agricultural worker is only about 5 *Taka* per day. Additional income obtained by corrupt means is therefore a matter of life or death for all workers. We would do better to avoid making judgements, as we tend to do, from a safe distance about the 'minor corruption' that goes on. It is often a direct result of hunger.[5]

In Thailand the price of rice doubled between August 1973 and July 1974. One kilo of pork rose from 16 to 35 *Baht* and one kilo of tuna fish from 6 to 22 *Baht* over the same period. The average income was 400 to 500 *Baht* per month and the daily income of an industrial worker was only 16 *Baht* (or 30 pence) a day. In Guatemala the legal minimum daily wage was 1 *Quetzal* in 1974. In the first six months of 1974 the prices for basic foodstuffs more than doubled. Maize went up from 4 to 9 *Centavos* per pound, beans and rice from 8 to 18 *Centavos* per pound and flour from 7 to 17 *Centavos* per pound. More and more people suffered from underfeeding. As there are no trade unions or farmers associations, and a high number of unemployed and under-employed, those who are most hit by the crisis cannot protect themselves. In Tondo, a slum quarter of Manila (the Philippine capital), the daily wage in 1974 was in many cases only 8 *Pesos*. Of the men of employable age 20 per cent were without work and many of the others were often only temporarily employed. One kilo of rice costs 2.90 *Pesos*. Just to cover its daily rice needs a family of six has to spend more than 8 *Pesos*. The authorities have calculated that the minimum expenditure for food in the first quarter of 1974 was 18.33 *Pesos* and they have put the total daily cost of living at 38.27.

Famine today is primarily a problem of poverty and insufficient buying power. For this reason it is an illusion to think it can be overcome merely by increasing production. Despite the recognised surplus of grain in India and her export of millions of tons to Bangladesh between 1971/72, the Indians had as little to eat as always.[6]

But even the United States herself had to reflect on the scandal of the 1960s — that in the middle of wealth and surplus 'every night more than ten million Americans went to bed hungry'. This remark, made by President Kennedy in 1963, has often been repeated. Official estimates suggest that towards the end of the 1960s, fifty million North Americans, i.e. a quarter of the population, were undernourished and twenty million were malnourished.[7] The causes have since been revealed as part of the socio-economic structure of the United States 'which suffers from unjust and inhumane exploitation and significant discrimination'.

The moral of this is self-evident: reports about increasing productivity tell us just as little about the real food situation as do the figures for average consumption per capita. For example in Brazil annual food production is growing 4.4 per cent — faster than the population growth rate of (3 per cent) and faster than domestic demand, which has a 4 per cent growth rate. The calorie requirement of 2,620 calories per person per day is in excess supply (110 per cent), and the protein supply of 65 grains is also theoretically met.

Nevertheless endemic undernourishment prevails in north-east Brazil, and the lowest strata of society suffer from severe underfeeding. In Recife more than half the children under five years die from malnutrition or its consequences.[8]

The decisive factor is not the *quantity* of available food, but its *distribution*. If the fight against famine is to be successful, then people must study the distribution mechanism; in other words, which part of the population is undernourished and why they are so must be understood. The fundamental causes are only attacked in very few countries, although the evidence from so many different countries conclusively shows that the lowest strata of society are the most underfed. Table 9 underlines the correlation between hunger and poverty.

Hunger is the visible biological end-product of an economic phenomenon — underdevelopment. Underdevelopment always implies inequality, discrepancy between production factors and supply and demand factors in diverse sectors of the population and in diverse regions. For this reason hunger can only be overcome by a radical change in the mechanism which produces underdevelopment. This not only implies social revolution, such as land reform, within developing countries themselves but also a reordering of international economic relations, for these have been the main or at least a significant cause of the unequal development between industrial countries and developing countries.

The Third World is accustomed to these relationships. Mexico's President, Luis Echeverria Alvarez, diagnosed it in a speech to the FAO Council on 9 February 1974:

The Third World can end up in open and irreversible crisis. It must not be forgotten that the right to food, the right to a life in dignity and the right to work are more than just words — they are active, historical expressions of the collective consciousness today in every part of the world. The dichotomy between the moral value of words and their innermost functional and practical being has been turned into a historical chasm that the peoples bridge as best they can: with anything from despair to utopia. This is why I have said that the basic question is obvious: either

Table 9: Daily food intake per capita in relation to income BRAZIL (1960)

Income	North-East Urban		North-East Rural		East Urban		East Rural		South Urban		South Rural	
Cruzeiros per house-hold/year	House-hold %	per Cap/Day Kilo Cals	House-hold %	per Cap/Day Kilo Cals	House-hold %	per Cap/Day Kilo Cals	House-hold %	per Cap/Day Kilo Cals	House-hold %	per Cap/Day Kilo Cals	House-hold %	per Cap/Day Kilo Cals
under 100	9	1240	18	1500	5	1180	7	1420	1	1480	4	2380
100-149	13	1500	14	1810	5	1530	10	2100	3	1740	4	2900
150-249	26	1500	25	2140	17	1880	20	2210	11	1970	16	2500
250-349	17	2320	13	1820	14	2090	15	2720	13	2050	15	2860
350-499	14	2420	10	2280	17	2220	13	2670	20	2360	18	2970
500-799	11	2860	11	2370	20	2630	13	2920	22	2470	21	3000
800-1199	5	3110	5	3380	11	2820	8	3060	14	2780	9	3780
1200-2499	4	4040	3	2870	9	3270	11	3040	12	3080	10	4360
over 2500	1	4290	1	2900	2	3750	3	4100	4	3170	3	4770

Source: *Food Consumption in Brazil, Family Budget Surveys in Early 1960s*, Getulio Vargas Foundation, Brazil 1970

Table 9 (continued)   PAKISTAN and BANGLADESH (1962-1966)

| Total Income | Pakistan | | | | Bangladesh | | | |
| | Urban | | Rural | | Urban | | Rural | |
	House-hold %	Kilo-Cals per Cap/Day	House-hold %	Kilo-Cals per Cap/Day	House-hold %	Kilo-Cals per Cap/Day	House-hold %	Kilo-Cals per Cap/Day
Rupees per household month								
under 99	25	1700	46	2000	19	1550	44	2050
100-199	38	1780	32	2140	25	1750	34	2260
200-299	15	1750	11	2200	19	1720	14	2400
300-399	7	1800	3	2460	10	1810	4	2660
400-499	4	2090	1	2110	8	1800	2	2640
over 500	7	1960	3	2460	19	1840	2	3060
unknown	4	1820	4	2350	–	–	–	–

Sources: *Nutrition Survey of West Pakistan: February 1965 to November 1966,*
   The Directorate of Nutrition and Research, Pakistan 1970
   East Pakistan Nutrition Survey 1962-63,
   The Directorate of Nutrition and Research, Pakistan 1965

Table 9 (continued)

INDIA (Maharastra 1971)

Income Rs/month per caput	per cent of households	Kcals per caput/day
-15	1	940
15-25	23	1540
25-35	26	1950
35-45	18	2240
45-55	15	2590
55-65	8	3150
65-75	5	110
75+	4	90

MADAGASCAR (Rural: 1962)

Income per household FMG per year	per cent of households	Kcals per caput/day
1-20	55	2150
20-40	28	2290
40-80	11	2250
80-130	4	2360
130-190	2	2350
190-390	1	2340
390-590	0.3	2360
other groups	0.2	—

TUNISIA (Rural: 1965-68)

Total expenditure Dinars per caput/year	per cent of households	Kcals per caput/day
less 20	8	1780
20-27	8	2120
27-32	8	2190
32-45	20	2430
45-53	11	2620
53-64	12	2750
64-102	20	2900
102-150	9	3180
150-200	2	3250
200+	2	3150

Sources: India: Unpublished source, Maharastra, 1971
Madagascar: *Budgets et alimentation des ménages ruraux en 1962,*
Ministère des Finances et du Commerce, Madagascar
Tunisia: *La consommation et les dépenses des ménages en Tunisie 1965-68,*
Secrétariat d'état au plan et à l'économie nationale, Tunisie, 1968

cooperation or world chaos. For solutions involving
containment by force are not only unjust, but impractical
in the present state of the new balance of power.[9]

Echeverria is one of the most important leaders of the Third
World. His diagnosis is so pertinent that it needs to be
elaborated, and one could add that his own rhetoric is as
applicable to Mexico as elsewhere. Not only is the world
divided, but the division within developing countries themselves — between the rich classes in power who have economic
interests in industrialised countries and the poor masses — is
deep and bitter. With various degrees of support from outside,
the ruling classes answer by crushing any liberation movements
of the suppressed and starving masses.

The unrest grows quickly and according to Gandhi's chief
follower, Jayaprahesh Narayan, the people 'found all the
doors to seek a redress to their grievances by legitimate and
democratic means completely shut'.[10] The doors in India
have been even more firmly shut and Narayan himself was in
prison for five months during 1975. Resistance from below
and repression from above are both escalating. Resistance is
usually in the form of spontaneous rebellion, since it is
almost impossible for people weak from hunger to organise
lengthy political campaigns or insurrection.

Mao Tse-tung at least has succeeded in putting hunger
behind him. His revolution has managed to achieve 'The
greatest wish the Chinese people have ever had' — the
liberation of China from starvation.

5   From food aid to world food security

Those developing countries most seriously affected by the increasing costs of oil and foods imported 12.5 million tons of grain in 1973/74, 17.5 million tons in 1974/75 and will need to import an estimated 14 to 18 million in 1975/76.[1] Using the same trends for production and demand it is estimated that the gap in supply for developing countries will, by 1985, reach between 70 and 85 million tons. That is the amount needed to feed 350 to 425 million people.[2]

There is only one rational course — to put every effort into raising production in the developing countries themselves. But even in the best circumstances a significant gap will still remain, which can only be filled by some kind of food aid programme. Already much of Africa and the Far East is dependent on this kind of assistance (see table 10).

The view that food aid will remain a constant necessity for years to come intensifies the already existing one-sided dependence of developing countries. The bilateral dependency in which the developing countries are currently caught up must be overcome through cooperation on the international level, so that the consequences of past experience do not reoccur. The reason we say this becomes apparent once we analyse the American 'Food for Peace' programme which provided 84 per cent of all food aid between 1965 and 1972.[3]

In 1954 the United States authorities passed a law, the Agricultural Trade Development and Assistance Act, Public Law 480 (from now on referred to as PL 480). The law was formulated to dispose of surplus cereal production resulting from contemporary agricultural policies.

Under *Title 1* food was sold at favourable conditions to governments in return for dollars or local goods and the governments were able to re-sell the food in their own countries. The largest share of the equivalent value (about

57

Table 10: Food aid as a percentage of grain imports[4]

All non-OPEC Developing Countries	20.4	1965
	40.0	1970
	30.8	1971
	28.6	1972
	16.6	1973
Africa (non-OPEC)	24.8	1965
	14.3	1970
	28.1	1971
	15.6	1972
	34.8	1973
Central and South America (non-OPEC)	7.1	1965
	23.2	1970
	3.3	1971
	12.3	1972
	3.2	1973
Near East (non-OPEC)	3.3	1965
	43.0	1970
	18.6	1971
	11.2	1972
	4.1	1973
Far East (non-OPEC)	30.1	1965
	53.0	1970
	58.5	1971
	50.6	1972
	26.0	1973

80 per cent) was given over to the receiver country as a gift or as a long-term loan on easy terms for development purposes or common defence aims.

Under *Title 2* the food went free to governments, aid organisations and the United Nations World Food Programme. It was used in food programmes for especially underprivileged groups: mothers and children in the 'Food for Work' programmes; for the improvement of infrastructures and for aid action in emergency situations (for example, the Sahel and Ethiopia).

PL 480 was a way of promoting the sale of American agricultural products outside the United States. Because the surpluses were valued outside the market system, price falls were avoided. In addition there were gains in foreign policy to be drawn from the programme and the food seemed to be well employed in the developing countries in the fight against hunger and malnutrition. George McGovern, the first president of the 'Food for Peace Programme' (the name given to the organisation by the State Department responsible for administering PL 480), has called the programme an ingenious combination of self-interest and idealism.[5]

Taken overall, the American food aid brought the developing nations substantial relief from the most urgent food problems. It also provided work for thousands of unemployed through the work programmes and an improvement of infrastructures through development projects. And not least it also eased the balance of payments problems of the developing nations, for in the 1960s 30 to 45 per cent of their total food imports were made up of food aid.

The crisis sharply throws into relief the unpleasant fact that the aid programmes have had the unfortunate by-product of encouraging Third World governments to rely on surplus production by the United States and to neglect their own agricultural production — an all too obvious temptation because in most cases an improvement in production would mean structural changes, which would jeopardise the privileges of their own influential upper class. Neglected reforms have only strengthened the bilateral dependence of the developing nations on the United States.

In 1959 in India the Congress Party tried to bring about some legislation on agricultural reform in order to increase production. However the right wing of the party decided on the easier option of buying huge quantities of grain under PL 480, which was a major cause of the stagnation of India's own development efforts. India paid for this in her increased dependency on the United States. In 1966 President Johnson began to impose conditions for further aid donations by forcing India to open her doors to American investment. India had to abandon her own programme for building fertiliser factories. Instead western petro-chemical concerns took over that task.[6]

Since 1972 the volume of food aid has shrunk, exactly at the moment when the increasing cost of living has put the developing countries in greatest jeopardy. In 1970, food aid totalled 6.1 million tons, in 1973 the total fell to 2.5 million and in 1974 it was less than 1 million. Between 1972 and 1974 the dollar value of food exported under Title 1 of PL 480 rose from 549 million to 640 million dollars. But because of price rises and increased costs the *actual amount* of food delivered in 1974 only represented one third of the 1972 programme.

Even so four countries in whom the United States is particularly interested on grounds of military security were able to double their share of supplies within one year. South Vietnam, Cambodia, Jordan and Israel received 63 per cent of the total Title 1 programme in 1974 (half the wheat supply, two thirds of the animal feedstuff cereals and the total rice supply).[7] Half the 1975 commitments came under Title 1. Chile, South Korea, Indonesia, Pakistan, Egypt, Jordan, Syria and Israel had the greatest priorities, while India, Bangladesh and Sri Lanka did not receive even a fifth of the total.[8] The supply of aid to Chile was initially requested by former President Salvador Allende. After his death the supply to the military junta approached the three-million-dollar mark. By 1975 this had risen to thirty-seven million dollars. Food aid followed after financial aid, once the stability of the regime was established.

The dollar value of the Title 2 programme sank from 380

million dollars in 1972 to an estimated 248 million dollars in 1974. Together with rising prices this resulted in a drastic reduction in the programme. Deliveries of wheat in 1974 were only half as high as the previous year, while rice and milk products disappeared from the programme altogether. For this reason twenty-six food aid programmes in developing countries had to be abandoned in 1973/74 and the number of people who benefited from food aid dropped from 74 to 55 million. During 1973 54 per cent of the programmes in thirty-two of the worst affected developing countries still existed. However by 1974 only 43 per cent of these programmes were being carried out.[9]

Power politics in a situation of tight supplies inevitably weigh much more heavily than humanitarian needs. America's response is no exception. The report of the Senate Committee on 'Nutrition and the International Situation' quoted an article in the *Alabama Star* as a typical American attitude:

On the face of it, nothing could be more altruistic and well-intended than our Food for Peace Program. We give food to peoples who need it. Nothing is more useful in a world suffering from spreading shortages of foodstuffs. But that's not the way the program works. In the first place, we only give away surplus foods that aren't needed by the American People. Hardly a national sacrifice, but fair enough. Then we dispense the surplus foods, not on the basis of where they are most needed, but on the basis of power/political considerations of foreign affairs. In other words, we use the food as ammunition. There has been a continuing struggle between the Department of State, which favors giving food to our military allies, and the Department of Agriculture, which prefers to use the food to develop future commercial markets for American business. Very little of our Food for Peace has gone to Africa, where tens of thousands have perished from famine: But during the last year nearly half of it went to Cambodia and South Vietnam.[10]

In late 1974, in an attempt to counter this realpolitik trend,

Congress put an upper limit of 30 per cent on the food aid under Title 1 which does not go to those worst-stricken developing countries.

From the analysis of the American food programme it has become all too obvious that such programmes should be largely multilateral and not depend on the presence of surpluses on the world market. The World Food Programme initiated by the United Nations in 1961 and administered by the FAO fulfils the first of these conditions. But because it depended for about 40 per cent of its means on US contributions from PL 480 since 1972 it had had to cut back its work dramatically.

The World Food Conference held in November 1974 therefore tried to enlarge the circle of donor countries in order to overcome this food aid problem. The aim was to arrange for ten million tons a year to be put at the disposal of the World Food Programme. Canada, Argentina, Japan, the Netherlands, New Zealand, Norway, the US and Yugoslavia have all increased their available contributions. With not too considerable an effort, this figure may be reached in 1975 — the first year since the Food Conference. By the end of June 1975 nine million tons of surplus was available. That was already double the amount for 1974 and three times as much as for the year 1973/74.[11]

The World Food Conference discussed further measures such as 'international commitment to the security of world food stocks'. These aimed at an internationally coordinated system, although grain stocks were to be administered at the nation level. By the end of June 1975 forty-three countries had joined in. But 85 per cent of all grain exports and more than half the world's grain imports did not fall under this programme. The Soviet Union and China were not keen on joining this 'international' group.[12]

Another outcome of the World Food Conference was a global information and early-warning system. There was to be a continuous watch on the food situation so that assistance measures could be put into operation before disaster set in — for instance early shipping of grain supplies to the needy areas. Russia and China have opted out of this system as well, which makes it even more difficult to predict how much grain there will be in the world trading system.

The resolutions of the World Food Conference and the current adherence to them leaves many questions still unanswered. Are national stocks alone enough to ensure that food aid is free of political strings? In the United States the pressure from the agricultural lobby is so great that there is no question for the foreseeable future that stocks will remain in the hands of private firms. Five of the largest of these concerns together control 90 per cent of the cereal exports.[13] Senator McGovern, the head of the Senate Committee on the food question, has come out strongly against commercially administered grain reserves. He writes:

> The contention that the world can have reserves held in private hands is fallacious on its face. Private traders are in business to turn investment into profit as rapidly as possible. To expect that a multiplicity of private traders would or should manage the acquisition and release of food and feed grains in a manner which will meet the goals of a conscious reserve policy — to flatten the widest upward and downward fluctuations in market prices and to maintain a steady supply against times of shortage — would be contradictory. . . In reality a reserve in private hands is no reserve at all. It is indeed precisely the same market mechanism which has produced the situation we face today.[14]

Food aid will have to exist for a long time to come. But if it is really to be a spur to development and not a hindrance it must be quickly reformed. The World Food Conference decisions are but a first step. We suggest in conclusion a few more:
1 The situation in which food aid is used to delay the adoption of essential reforms in developing countries must be avoided. The highest priority is to increase the potential for self-sufficiency and autarchy.
2 Food aid must not prevent the growth in home production and in the domestic market.

3 Food aid should assist developing countries in adapting from their export-orientated production to an agriculture which is primarily concerned with domestic needs and the improvement of the diet of the poorest inhabitants. Food aid would make good the deficits in home production.
4 Aid programmes should guarantee that food reaches those with greatest need. A country which is unable to ensure that this happens should only receive assistance when the prevailing structure is altered.
5 Food aid should guarantee that the 'Food for Work' programme aims to improve the agricultural infrastructure in the form of land reform policies. This should also increase domestic employment and ensure that the benefits do not all accrue to the rich overseers.

The World Food Conference produced the mechanism for future international cooperation on such vital issues. But it has yet to be seen whether its resolutions will really work and whether the conference helped the hungry masses or merely appeased those already satisfied.

6 Migration, urbanisation and income inequality

Whatever is done to resolve the immediate crisis, there looms the larger question of how do we develop a world that is continuously on the edge of the abyss of disaster? Because the crisis in food production and distribution is but one warning light indicating that something is going seriously wrong. Once we begin to dismantle the engine of economic development we find at least three other major faults. There is the phenomenon of numbers of new proletarians swarming off an overcrowded unsupporting land into cities built to receive but a twentieth or a fortieth of the number. And from this problem is born yet another — unemployment and under-employment. In some Third World countries unemployment rates run as high as 40 per cent. Then there is the problem of income distribution. All the indications are that when there has been rapid economic growth and urbanisation, the new wealth instead of easing the social condition has worsened it — increasing the disparities between men; indeed in some countries even making the poor poorer.

What we plan to do in this chapter is to look at these 'mechanical faults' in turn. Then in the next chapter we shall examine an alternative — a new machine based on the dynamics of rural development.

In the fifty years, 1920-1973, the number of persons engaged in agriculture in the developing world almost doubled. It increased from approximately 240 million to 450 million. In the same space of time the acreage of agricultural land increased by only a quarter.

It is not surprising then, given the low level of technical expertise in the countryside and the increasing awareness, thanks to the transistor radio, of the 'glories' of the town, that hundreds of thousands of people have flocked from their villages into the city.

65

Between 1920 and 1960 the urban population of the Third World rose at an annual rate of 4 per cent. This is twice the rate in the developed countries during their time of development (see table 11).

Table 11: Annual average rates of growth of the urban population and increase in the rate of urbanisation (percentages)

Region and country	1850-1920	1920-60	1960-2000
Growth of the urban population			
Developing countries with market economies	—	4.0	4.1
Africa	—	4.3	4.6
America	—	4.4	4.2
Asia	—	3.8	4.0
Developed countries	2.5	1.9	1.7
Europe	1.9	1.3	1.1
USSR	—	4.0	2.6
North America	4.3	2.2	2.0
Increase in the rate of urbanisation [1]			
Developing countries with market economies	—	2.3	1.6
Africa	—	2.6	1.9
America	—	2.1	1.2
Asia	—	2.2	1.6
Developed countries	1.5	1.1	0.8
Europe	1.2	0.6	0.5
USSR	—	3.2	1.4
North America	2.1	0.8	0.5

[1] Rate of urbanisation: percentage of the total population living in agglomerations of over 20,000 inhabitants.

Sources: after 1920, United Nations: Growth of the world's urban and rural population, 1920-2000, prior to 1920, the author's calculations, in Paul Bairoch, *Urban unemployment in developing countries* (ILO, Geneva 1973)

In the 1850s, when 15 per cent of Europe's population was living in towns the annual rate of increase of urbanisation was 1.2 per cent. In the developing countries at around the same stage of development — the 1950s — the rate was 2.6 per cent.

In some Third World countries the pace of transition between countryside and town reaches almost breathtaking proportions. Take the case of Brazil. As recently as 1950 Brazil was still a predominantly agrarian nation with about 64 per cent of its people living in the countryside. But fifteen years later the rural and urban populations were about the same. And by 1970 the census found that only 44 per cent of the country's 93 million people were left on the farms. Between 1960 and 1970 10 million people migrated and the urban population mushroomed by 5.2 per cent a year. And that together with natural increase took the town population up to 21 million. At the end of the decade one quarter of Brazil's population was concentrated in nine large metropolitan areas.

The Third World countryside has been neglected. Family size grows, feudal land ownership systems remain untouched despite millions of words of reforming legislation, agricultural techniques are primitive. The markets for cash crops unstable and fluctuating and governments give low priority to agricultural development. Between 1920 and 1960 the Latin American work force grew by nearly 54 million. Farming, however, offered only 12 million new jobs.

Even when there is opportunity in the countryside, the young men often find the town more appealing. An adolescent is bound to earn more in a town job than he could hope to earn at home until he is old enough to farm independently. And by the time he has reached that age he has lost his attachment to the land. The fact is not only will a job give him a higher income but as Dr Caroline Hutton[1] showed in her revealing study of Kampala's unemployed, they feel that in the town they have a chance of an income that will not depend on weather or market prices and will be paid regularly week by week.

Urban growth in the Third World, writes Barbara Ward, has

become pathological.[2] In 1920, 185 million people in the more developed countries lived in towns over 20,000; 80 million of these in the big cities. For the less developed lands the figures were 68 million townsmen and only 16 million in big cities. By 1980, assuming present trends continue, cities in the Third World will have 100 million more inhabitants than the developed cities, and 70 per cent of them will be living in the big cities.

The European relationship between urbanisation and industrialisation has been turned on its head. European cities, horrible as they often are, at least had a purpose. They grew to fuel economic activity. European cities grew because of the industrial revolution: the subdivision of work into a myriad of tasks. And the subdivision created simultaneously increased productivity, the services to finance and distribute the new found wealth and an ever increasing demand for labour. But the cities of the developing world have grown ahead of industrialisation. In nineteenth-century Europe the proportion of the population living in cities of over 20,000 was always less than the working force engaged in manufacturing. In France in 1856, 10.7 per cent of the population was living in the urban areas and 29 per cent working in industry. In Sweden in 1890 the proportions were 10.8 per cent and 22 per cent. In Switzerland in 1888 even more startlingly, 45 per cent of the labour force were already in manufacturing but a mere 13 per cent of its people were town dwellers. Compare this with what is going on in today's developing world. In Tunis in 1956, 17.5 per cent of the people were in cities, but only 6.8 per cent of the labour force was in industry. In Brazil in 1960, 28.1 per cent in cities, 9.5 per cent in industry. Although the economic growth of Venezuela has been a remarkable 10 per cent a year, the number of unemployed at the end of a decade of fast expansion is as high as ever. Cities like Dakar and Abidjan with populations approaching a million have nearly half the country's population living in them. Yet a mere 5 per cent of their population is engaged in industry. But the causes of this imbalance are more complex than might first appear: it is not merely that industrialisation is in its infancy in the Third World, it is the kind of

Table 12: Comparison of the levels of urbanisation and of the percentages of the active population engaged in manufacturing

Region and year	Urban population rate	Percentage of the active population in manufacturing	Difference between two previous columns
Europe[2](excl. England)			
1850	11.0	16.0	− 30
1880	16.0	18.0	− 10
1900	24.0	20.0	+ 20
1920	29.0	21.0	+ 40
1930	32.0	22.0	+ 45
Developing countries with market economies			
1920	6.7	8.5	− 20
1930	7.8	8.5	− 10
1940	9.7	8.0	+ 20
1950	12.9	7.5	+ 70
1960	16.7	9.0	+ 85
1970	19.7	10.0	+100
1970[3]	21.0	10.0	+110
Africa 1960	13.4	7.0	+ 90
America 1960	32.8	14.5	+125
Asia 1960	13.7	9.0	+ 50

[1] To the nearest unit for the urban population rates and the percentages of the active population in Europe: to the nearest half-unit for the percentages of the active population in the developing countries and to the nearest five units for the differences. [2] Excluding the USSR. [3] The author's estimates see Bairoch, Urban Unemployment in developing countries.
Source: Bairoch

industrialisation that is being introduced. Manufacturing increased at an average rate of between 6 and 7 per cent between 1960 and 1970, faster indeed than the rate of increase in most of the now industrialised countries when they were developing. Manufacturing today accounts for 17 per cent of the combined GNP of the developing countries compared with 12 per cent twenty years ago. This surge of economic progress however does not spill over into the unemployment pool. Manufacturing absorbed less than one-fifth of the approximate 200 million increase in the labour force between 1950 and 1970. The annual increase in job opportunities averaged a mere 4 per cent.

Much of the fault lies in the imported capital intensive technology that is used in the Third World — using techniques from advanced economies in which physical capital is relatively abundant and in which labour is in short supply. There are good reasons and bad reasons why this should be so. The good reasons are that this is the only kind of machinery one can buy these days — or at least get in a regular supply of spare parts and servicing for. Also those projects using larger quantities of capital, it is argued, are those yielding high rates of profits to wages. And profits can be ploughed back to increase growth. The bad list is longer. At the top of it is the 'prestige factor': the feeling rife in too many poor countries that in order to create a 'modern' society they should emulate us. In Uganda, to take a not untypical example, investing firms can write off 120 per cent of capital expenditure against tax, but there are no inducements offered to maximise employment. And multinational corporations who make up much of the new investment in the developing countries demand this kind of treatment, threatening to invest elsewhere if they do not receive it. A recent UN study listed some of the problems posed by multinationals:

'Multinational corporations often concentrate on higher technology industries employing capital intensive techniques. Although such industries may contribute to the eventual modernization of the industrial structure of the host countries, They may not serve one of the immediate prime objectives of development, namely an increase in employment opportunities.

'Furthermore, many of the products which multinational corporations specialize in cater to the demand in high income countries. When they are marketed in developing countries, they may introduce patterns of consumption which are not conducive to sustained development and confer very limited benefits to the vast majority of the population.'[3]

Foreign aid often exacerbates the process. 90 per cent of American aid is tied; 48 per cent of British. What this means is that aid must be spent on imports from the donor country. Rarely is aid allowed for local costs. So, perversely, it becomes cheaper for an aid receiving country building a road to use imported earthmoving equipment than to use men with picks and shovels.

The result of all this is that industry, instead of providing a favourable demonstration of the possibilities of development, too often undermines local initiative. E F Schumacher calls it 'a process of mutual poisoning'. He writes: 'the establishment of modern industry in a few metropolitan areas tends to kill off competing types of traditional production throughout the countryside, thus causing widespread unemployment or under-employment. The countryside thereupon takes its revenge by mass migration into the metropolitan areas causing them to grow to a totally unmanageable size.'[4]

A frighteningly high proportion of these new proletarians-to-be end up in the towns without a job, and often without a roof.

A study by the international Labour Office provides a startling portrait of urban unemployment.[5]

The number of unemployed in urgan agglomerations of 20,000 or more inhabitants has grown as follows: 1950, 8 million; 1960, 13 million; 1970, 24 million. Unemployment in the urban areas of Africa averages 27 per cent; in the Philippines 13 per cent; in Bogota, Colombia 11 per cent. In the table below one third of countries have unemployment rates of over 15 per cent. In two thirds of the countries it exceeds 8 per cent.

But to see the full danger of these figures they should be compared with Europe when it was developing. In Britain between 1851 and 1910 unemployment did not normally

Table 13: Rates of urban and rural unemployment (percentages of the active population)

Country	Year	Urban unemployment	Rural unemployment
AFRICA			
Algeria	1966	26.6	—
Burundi	1963[1]	18.7[2]	—
Cameroon	1964[1]	4.6	3.4
"	1966	15.0[3]	—
Ghana	1960	11.6	—
Ivory Coast[1]	1963	20.0	—
Morocco	1960	20.5	5.4
Nigeria	1963	12.6	—
Tanzania	1965	7.0	3.9
Zaire	1967	12.9[2]	—
AMERICA			
Argentina	1968	5.4[2]	—
Bolivia	1966	13.2[3]	—
Chile	1968	6.1	2.0
Colombia	1967	15.5[3]	—
Costa Rica	1966-67	5.6[2]	—
El Salvador	1961	6.6[2]	—
Guatemala	1964	5.4[2]	—
Guyana	1965	20.5[2]	—
Honduras	1961	7.8[2]	—
Jamaica	1960	19.0[2]	12.4[4]
Netherlands Antilles	1966	16.0[3]	—
Panama	1960	15.5	3.6
"	1967	9.3	2.8
Peru	1964	4.2[2]	—
"	1969	5.2[2]	—
Uruguay	1963	10.9	2.3
Venezuela	1961	17.5	4.3
"	1964	16.4[3]	—
"	1968	6.5	3.1

Table 13 (continued)

ASIA			
India[5]	1961-62	3.2	1.7[5]
Indonesia	1961	8.5	—
Iran	1956	4.5	1.8
"	1966	5.5	11.3
Korea	1963-64	7.0	1.8
Malaysia (west)	1967	11.6	7.4
Philippines	1967	13.1	6.9
Singapore	1966	9.1	—
Sri Lanka	1959-60	14.3	10.0
Syrian Arab Republic	1967	7.3	—
Thailand	1966	2.8[3]	—

[1] Men only. [2] Capital city only. [3] Average (weighted by size of population) for a certain number of main towns. [4] Excluding capital city. [5] Account taken of the adjustment suggested by Turnham for improving the comparability of the two rates.

Sources: mainly Turnham, op. cit., pp. 57 and 134-135 together with the following:

L S Moulin and M Ducreux: 'Le Phénomène urbain à Kinshasa: évolution et perspectives', Etudes congolaises (Kinshasa), No. 4, Oct. — Dec. 1969;

Kwan S.Kim: 'Labour force structure in a dual economy: a case study of South Korea', International Labour Review, Vol. 101, No. 1, Jan. 1970, pp. 35-48;

Irv Beller: 'Latin America's unemployment problem', Monthly Labor Review (Washington, DC, US Department of Labor), Vol. 93, No. 11, Nov. 1970, pp. 3-10 (for Peru, 1969);

R Clignet: 'Preliminary notes of a study of unemployment in modern African urban centers', Manpower and Underemployment Research in Africa, Vol. 2, No. 1, Apr. 1969, pp. 28-32 (for Cameroon, 1966);

'The unemployment problem in Latin America' (Washington DC, Organization of American States, 1969), quoted by Ralph H. Hofmeister: 'Growth with unemployment in Latin America: some implications for Asia', in Ridker and Lubell, op. cit., Vol. II, pp. 819-848 (for Venezuela, 1964);

ILO: Rapport au gouvernement du Royaume du Burundi sur l'emploi et le chômage à Usumbura (Geneva, 1964).

exceed 6 to 7 per cent. On rare occasions at a time of economic crisis it may have reached 15-20 per cent.[6] In Germany the figures were lower. Between 1887 and 1914 unemployment averaged only 2.4 per cent.[7]

What is most disturbing about these Third World unemployment figures is that the burden of them falls on the young. Men at an age when they are at their most ambitious, most yearning, even most idealistic period of their lives are subject to the humiliation of having failed. Nothing is more likely to sow the seeds of strife and discontent. In three out of the eighteen countries mentioned in table 13 unemployment among the 15-24 year olds is 40 per cent or more; in six countries it is between 20 and 29 per cent. Only in four countries does the rate fall below 10 per cent.

Underemployment is even worse. In a developed economy an expanding tertiary sector is a sign of progress — services are the harvest of economic achievement. Quite the reverse in Latin America, Asia and Africa — services are parasites drawing odd coins from the casual passage of wealthier pockets. Shoe shine boys, sellers of ticky tacky, messages, cigarette vendors, tourist touts, porters eke out a living contributing only marginally to economic development. The proportion of the non-agricultural labour force engaged in services in Latin American countries is between 60 and 70 per cent; in Europe it is between 40 and 50 per cent.[8] And in 1910 at a time when Europe had a general level of income equivalent to Latin America in 1960, the tertiary sector employed only 22-23 per cent of the active population.

This is a disease that economic growth probably cannot cure. It is too pathological, too far gone, for the urban industrial treatment to have any effect.[9]

In an attempt to show just how impossible the situation is an OECD study has made the following calculation. It takes the average situation prevailing in the developing countries: a manufacturing sector employing 20 per cent of the labour force; the unemployment rate and underemployment rate together average 25 per cent, the increase in labour productivity is assumed to be 2.5 per cent a year, the rate achieved between 1955 and 1968.

It then calculates that in order to absorb an increase in the labour force growing at 3 per cent a year (it is in fact growing at 4 per cent) industrial production would have to increase at the phenomenal rate of 18 per cent a year. (Even record breaking Brazil has only achieved 15 per cent.) And to eradicate within a decade the existing rural and urban unemployment and underemployment it would have to increase by 30-35 per cent a year. Even to match productivity increases and thus maintain a constant labour force in manufacturing a 3 per cent growth per annum in output is needed. The report not surprisingly concludes 'Thus eradication of general underemployment through the development of industrial employment is a practical impossibility in the medium term.'[10] And in an ominous footnote we are told 'in some African countries manufacturing employment seems to have been falling'. Robert McNamara adds to the gloom surrounding the problem. He writes:

> For employment to grow at a rate of 4.5 per cent per year in the urban areas of the developing world would be a tremendous achievement, beyond anything that has been achieved in the past (yet) a 4.5 per cent growth in urban jobs would provide work for an increase in the total rural and urban labour force of 1.3 per cent, or approximately one half of the increase anticipated.[11]

And so the favelas, callampas, barriades and bidonvilles will continue to proliferate. Already in Calcutta the number of people living in one room is 79 per cent of the population. Large numbers live on the pavement. In Caracas 30 per cent of the population live in shanty towns; in Lima 20 per cent, in Buenos Aires 10 per cent.

Sanitation and sewerage systems cannot cope. Djakarta has a population of nearly five million, but it has no sewerage, no safe running water and few transport services. In Brazil only 45 per cent of the municipalities have reliable water supplies. Only 34 per cent have sewerage systems. In 1971 only 38 per cent of Latin American towns had sewerage services. Even that was up from 28 per cent in 1961.

Although the conclusion is clear — the town cannot usefully employ these millions of people and if it cannot employ them it cannot house them either — they continue to pour in. It is likely that by 1980 Latin America will have a population of 358 million. 60 per cent of these, 218 million, will be living in the cities. This will mean an increase of the urban population of 100 million — equivalent to all of Brazil's population — within the short space of fifteen years. In 1960 there were nine cities in eight Latin American countries with over one million inhabitants. In 1980 there will be twenty-seven cities of this size.[12]

Given overwhelming pressures on Third World cities it is not surprising to see large numbers of their young men emigrating overseas — South Koreans to Japan, Mexicans to the United States, Turks, Algerians and West Indians to Western Europe. Excluding intra EEC migrants, there are ten million immigrants in Common Market Europe alone — about the same number as the combined population of three member countries: Denmark, Ireland and Luxembourg. A UN forecast (pre oil crisis) estimated a total immigrant labour force of twenty-two million by 1980. That would be nearly half as many as emigrated from Europe to the New World in the great nineteenth and early twentieth century migrations. As we know those American migrations produced enormous turbulence and suffering. But relative to what is happening today, that was a homogenous migration. By far and away the overwhelming majority of immigrants were of European stock and Judaeo-Christian culture. Now we have Turks, Moroccans, Jamaicans, Algerians, Pakistanis, Surinames, Greeks, Yugoslavs, Antilleans, South Koreans, Filipinos moving into the bottom rungs of a society totally different in conception and mores. Strangeness, antagonism, withdrawal, hostility, reaction are feeding on each other. The fragments of violence proliferate.

But Europe now finds it difficult to dispense with its immigrants. This plentiful supply of relatively undemanding labour, young and hardworking, has favoured a degree of economic development that would have been impossible without them. They have increased productivity by removing labour bottlenecks and have encouraged capital investment by being prepared to work nightshifts. They have kept wage levels from rising too fast and at the same time have enabled European workers to move into higher skilled jobs. They have made fewer demands on the social services because of their age structure and they have been prepared because of their mobility to move in and out of short-life jobs.

It looks at first sight as if this safety valve of migrations has much to commend it from the sending countries' point of view. An essay in the World Bank magazine *Finance and Development*[13] pointedly illustrated the benefit by showing that it would cost the rich countries sixty billion dollars in aid to create the same number of jobs in the sending countries as are filled by imported workers in Europe.

However, although there is an undoubted short-term value in relieving the pressure of urbanisation and population in the poor countries, in the long run this outflow is likely to be regretted.

All the evidence suggests that once the young men leave their villages, agrarian life becomes even more depressed. The farm work is left to the old and to the women. Agricultural production declines even further and the pressure for a second generation of migrants to leave becomes stronger.

It is too often blithely assumed that because Europe's present-day immigrants send home 2.5 billion dollars a year this is unanswerably a good thing. The study *Colour and Citizenship*[14], that 800-page result of five years of British liberal scholarship, gives only a dozen lines to the impact on the developing countries. 'Remittances', it says, 'have brought great improvements to the land and to the villages.' But it produces no evidence to substantiate its case.

Israel is occasionally cited as an example of a country where remittances have been remarkably helpful in aiding economic development. But Israel of course, in its stage of development, cannot be compared with the countries we are writing about. Consumer values were well advanced from the beginning. Its agricultural sector, led by kibbutz idealists, did not need to worry about holding people on the land; and its industrial sector was quickly established.

There is a darker picture in Hugh Brody's detailed and careful study of the west of Ireland[15], where emigration has cut the population by more than half. He recounts how, years ago, people would take turns to help each other with the harvest. There would be ceilidhs or celebrations in the evening in the house of whoever had been helped that day. This way of living lightened the drudge of the heavy agricultural work, but migration and remittances have broken this down. Families now feel more self-interested. The postal orders come from America or from Britain, and no one wants to tell anyone else how much they are getting. 'The displacement of cooring (communal work)', Brody writes, 'and all the sociability of mutual aid has left each household in extraordinary isolation.' Observers of the Irish agricultural scene point to a devastatingly destructive individualism that makes even the simplest co-operative venture — like building a road along a line of cottages — extraordinarily difficult. Remittances force a withdrawal; heavy drinking (and bricklaying too) often becomes its only external manifestation. Reports from other countries make similar observations. A survey in Portugal reveals that 32 per cent of remittances are spent on consumer items and domestic appliances, 24 per cent on education for the children, and 38 per cent on purchases of land and housing.

Another major part of the argument in favour of remittances has been the suggestion that they help the balance of payments, often a crucial impediment to growth in developing countries. But here again the evidence seems to overpower the wishful thinking.

Professor Nikolinakos' study of Greek/German exchanges[16] showed that the familiarisation of Greek migrants working in Germany (and the Greek public at large) with German goods led to a surprising situation, in which the increasing volume of remittance covered a decreasing proportion of the growing trade deficit. This paradoxical problem has been summed up by Roger Böhning, who is the International Labour Office's chief expert on migration:

Mechanically adding remittances to the trade deficit makes even less sense than mechanically subtracting emigrants from the unemployed, quite apart from the possible inflationary repercussions of such an inflow of disposable income. On the individual level, remittances are used in the first instance to cater for daily needs or to pay off old debts. A continuing inflow subsequently goes on consumer goods, sometimes of quite a fancy kind and often of foreign origin. None of this expenditure is more than marginally productive. Moreover, when the migrant extends his stay abroad and possibly sends for his family the remittances begin to dry up.

In macro-economic terms, the foreign currency tends to be used, wherever there is no strict control of imports, to pay for imports of foreign consumer goods by the non-migrant population and by recipients of remittances. Thus, there is an increasing familiarisation with foreign consumer goods brought about by publicity surrounding migration and by the emigrants themselves. It leads in effect to a widespread disdain for domestic products and a higher value placed on foreign goods. And it leaves little if any room for domestic productive investment.[17]

But if remittances are not what they are made out to be, then surely the fact that a returned emigrant comes home with new skills and experience is an undeniable asset in the development of a primitive industrial economy?

Madeleine Trebous, whose study of Algerian workers in France is the most comprehensive and detailed work on a migrant community, has attempted to answer this question.[18] Algeria is typical of many poor countries in the European orbit. In 1930 the country's urban population was 300,000 — about 5 per cent of the total. By 1960, however, it had risen to 25 per cent, by 1963 to 33 per cent; in 1966 it was 38 per cent. Rural population in this time almost doubled. Underemployment in 1963 was 49 per cent for Algeria as a whole and 64 per cent among the active urban population. The Algerian Plan Directorate, although allowing for the continuation of 300,000 jobs overseas, calculates that it needs between now and 1980 to create 60,000 to 80,000 jobs a year outside agriculture just to stay abreast of itself.

The Algerian migration to France is an old one. It began in 1871 with the departure of farm labourers and small urban tradesmen. In 1912 an official survey counted 4,000 to 5,000 Algerians in France 'engaged in laborious tasks in soapworks and the docks, especially in Marseilles'. Since 1945 the migratory movement had grown rapidly. Between 1948 and 1958 some 200,000 Algerians arrived in France. There are now 800,000 (including family members). According to the Plan Directorate's figures, roughly a quarter of the active Algerian population in permanent employment was away in Europe in 1966.

Today the Algerians tend to find work in the larger industrial firms in the major cities. At Renault's Billancourt works at the beginning of 1965, all the applicants for the thousands of jobs to be filled were foreigners. 'The French worker', as Marc Ouin of Renault told us, 'has an adverse image of industry. He'd rather have a white collar job, even if it's less well paid.' Renault employs 95,000 workers in its French plants, and of these 21,000 are immigrants. Increasingly the Algerians are beginning to move up the economic ladder. The proportion of Algerian skilled workers has more than doubled in fifteen years. Between 1953 and 1968 the number rose from 5.3 per cent of the total to 11.1 per cent.

One would hope that, after a period of work in France, these increasingly skilled and knowledgeable industrial workers will return home to furnish much-needed experience as Algerian industrial expansion begins to shift gears. Certainly their links with the homeland are stronger than, say, Commonwealth immigrants in Britain (not least because they are deterred by having to live for five years in France before being able to apply for citizenship). Attitude surveys show the Algerian would 'rather have a job in Algeria than in France' even if it means settling for a lower wage. Yet the reality of the situation, according to Madeleine Trebous, is more complex. There is a gross imbalance between the kind of job Algerians are doing in France and the kind of jobs that are being opened up back home. Two out of every three Algerian workers in Europe are employed in building and construction. Assuming Algeria carries out its planned vocational training of workers in the building, metal-working and transport sectors, about 70 per cent of the workers trained in Europe may not be able to find a job in Algeria unless they change their trade or obtain a higher level of skills. Yet the jobs that are likely to show unfilled vacancies in Algeria — in chemicals, hydrocarbons and textiles — are simply not the industries in which Algerians are employed in large numbers in France.

Inevitably, given the dictates of this situation (and it is repeated in all the sending countries), the immigrants are lengthening their stay in Europe. They are asking their families to join them, and although they keep on talking of 'going home', they rarely do, except for holidays.

'The migrant then, is constantly torn [Böhning writes] between his desire to overcome his deprivations and his desire to return home to a social context where he must feel the deprivations even more deeply than when he left. The result is that again and again he extends his stay abroad, and he re-emigrates repeatedly after returning home for a short while. Finally the process will lead to a significant number of target workers tending to settle down in the receiving country if not for ever, at least until retirement age.'

The impact of these elements on the developing countries is not an attractive one. Aspirations are raised; the agricultural economy undermined; balance of payments benefits are minimally affected, if at all; and enterprising families are lost indefinitely to a foreign economy.

One of the most widely held beliefs among economic

thinkers, until relatively recently, was the view that the most effective way to raise the populace's incomes was through rapid industrialisation. But as we have shown already large amounts of labour are not that easily given work. And there is increasing evidence that even when it is employed it only occurs in a situation where income distribution becomes severely skewed.

Mahub ul Haq, who used to be the Chief Economist with the Pakistan Planning Commission and who is now with the World Bank, has written about how the economic plans of fast growth rate countries are often made:

... looking at the national plans of the developing countries, it was obvious that employment was often a secondary, not a primary, objective of planning. It was generally added as an after-thought to the growth target in GNP but very poorly integrated in the framework of planning. Recalling my own experience with formulation of Pakistan's five year plans — the chapter on employment strategy was always added at the end, to round off the plans and make them look complete and respectable, and was hardly an integral part of the growth strategy of policy framework. In fact, most of the developments which affected the employment situation favourably such as the rural works programme and the green revolution, were planned primarily for higher output, and their employment-generating potential was accidental and not planned. There were endless numbers of research teams, our own and foreign, fixing up our national accounts and ensuring that they adequately registered our rate of growth; there was not a fraction of this effort devoted to employment statistics.

The employment objective, in short, has been the step-child of planning, and it has been assumed, far too readily, that high rates of growth will ensure full employment as well. But what if they don't? A sustained 6 per cent rate of growth in Pakistan in the 1960's led to rising unemployment, particularly in East Pakistan.[19]

Haq goes on to point out that not only did unemployment increase, but real wages in the industrial sector declined by one third. Per capita income disparity between east and west Pakistan nearly doubled and 'the concentration of industrial wealth became an explosive economic and political issue. And in 1968, while the intellectual world was still applauding Pakistan as a model of development, the system exploded — not only for political reasons but for economic unrest.'

So now after two decades of testing the industrial growth strategy in real life laboratories there is a growing awareness that all is not so straightforward.

Mexico, like Pakistan, has been regarded as one of the development successes: its GNP has risen by 6 or 7 per cent annually for the past fifteen years. But government policy has had a hefty bias toward the urban sector and large farms and again, like Pakistan, unemployment has been on the up and income disparities have worsened.

Between 1950 and 1969 the average per capita income grew in real terms by 3 per cent a year. The richest 10 per cent of the population received 49 per cent of the total national income at the beginning of this period and 51 per cent at the end. Meanwhile the poor got less. In 1950 the bottom 40 per cent received 14 per cent of the income pie. By 1969 it was down to 11 per cent. The poorest 20 per cent saw their share of the pie cut from 6 per cent to 4 per cent.[20]

India for all its attempts to socialise its economy, through a large state-run industrial sector, still has 40 per cent of its entire population — some 200 million people — below the poverty line — the level at which serious malnutrition is believed to exist. The World Bank believes that the poorest 10 per cent of the population — a not insignificant fifty million people — may have even grown poorer.

Yet for all the accumulating evidence against the panacea of fast growth based on the industrial sector it would not be fair to damn it without a close look at what has happened in Brazil. It is certainly in a statistical sense a remarkable success story.

The 10 per cent increase in GDP in 1974 made it the third consecutive year in which the growth of the Brazilian economy has exceeded 10 per cent. It was the sixth year in which it has topped 9 per cent. The average rate of growth of 10.2 per cent over 1967-73 has resulted in a 50 per cent increase in average net individual incomes. During these six years manufacturing output has doubled and merchandise exports have grown from US $1.7 billion to over $6 billion.

Brazil, with its population of close on 100 million, now has a larger national economy than any other western hemisphere country, bar the United States and Canada. No other developing country comes near to imitating its successful growth rate. The down town areas of Sao Paulo and Rio de Janeiro give a visual impression of being wealthier and more developed than any European city and indeed more than any North American city, save perhaps New York, Los Angeles and Chicago.

Yet for all its glitter and glory the average per capita income of this massive giant is a mere $600, making it one of the poorer Latin American countries. And the evidence appears to suggest that during this time of high growth income distribution has dramatically worsened.

The richest 10 per cent of the population appropriated almost three quarters of the gain in income between 1960 and 1970; the poorest 50 per cent took less than a tenth. Those with university education experienced a rise in income of 52 per cent, while the half of the population with some primary education had an income increase of only 14 per cent. The Minister of Finance himself has admitted that in the early years of this surge of growth 'it is probable that betwen 1964 and 1967 the (wage) formula provoked a certain compression of real wages'. And the World Bank has found that 'the share of the net income received by the poorest 40 per cent, declined from 10 per cent in 1960 to 8 per cent in 1970.'[21]

The distinguished American economist Albert Fishlow, who has made what is widely regarded as the outstanding evaluation of Brazilian income distribution, has observed:

to bring the lowest decile in the 1970 income distribution up to a minimum standard of living will take a continuing growth rate of 5 per cent annually for 20 years. That assumes the present income distribution remains unchanged. If it continues to worsen, as present policies do little to forestall, the time required could easily involve another decade. Can the present starving poor be expected to wait around for 30 years amid rising affluence to attain the princely sum of $100 per capita?[22]

Fishlow's criticisms are shared by an increasing number of economists both inside and outside Brazil. Yet the Brazilian policy makers stand firm. The Minister of Finance has argued that those who favour more equality are engaging in 'a veritable confidence game which could end up leaving the nation dividing misery more equitably'.

In reply Fishlow says that it would require only 6.1 per cent of the income of those above the poverty standard to be transferred to those below it to bring them up to the minimum. (The poverty line is $480 (1973 prices) for a family of five in the rural north-east and $690 in the urban south and east.)

Fishlow argues — and this is the nub of the debate — that 'such a redistribution of income would allow ample scope for continuing the incentive effects of differential rewards'.

Robert McNamara has taken up the same argument in a thinly veiled attack on the Brazilian government when at the Unctad conference in Santiago in April 1972 he said:

It is often suggested that wide disparities in income are necessary in order to provide entrepreneurial incentives. Without arguing whether such incentives are important stimuli to productivity, one can question the amount of incentive that is required to motivate the desired degree of effort. In a study of the income disparities of 39 developing countries, in which the income of the wealthiest 6 per cent of the population is measured as a multiple of the bottom 40 per cent, there is a wide range of differences among countries. In 8 of the 39 countries the per capita income of the top 5 per cent is

Table 14: Distribution of income in Brazil adjusted for consumption requirements

Multiple of poverty level[1]	Percentage of persons with family incomes in specified range	Percentage of income
0	.9	0.0
0 – 1/4	.8	.1
1/4 – 1/2	7.8	1.4
1/2 – 3/4	11.4	3.3
3/4 – 1	12.8	5.1
1 – 3/2	20.3	11.4
3/2 – 2	13.6	10.8
2 – 3	14.2	15.7
3 +	18.3	52.2

Mean income: 2.19 times the poverty line

[1] The unit of account is the poverty line, which varies for individual families by size, composition, region and location of residence. It thus incorporates the influence of these variables and adjusts for consumption requirements. The basic poverty standard to which these adjustments are made is the 1960 minimum wage in the north-east for a family between four and five persons. Actual family income is expressed as a multiple of the relevant poverty level.

more than 30 times greater than that of the lowest 40 per cent. In 16 countries the ratio is less than 15 to 1. (In the United States, the ratio is 5 to 1.)

The significant point is that when one compares these two sets of countries on the basis of their per capita growth performance during the 1960's there is no discernible relationship between the size of the incentives and the rapidity of growth. The average rate of growth of the group of countries with the greatest disparities was not significantly different from the group with the least. This indicates that there may well be substantial scope in the developing countries for moderating the highly skewed disparities in income without crippling the incentives to greater productivity.

Yet for all the evidence against the Brazilian way of doing things it would be foolish to underestimate the force of the arguments on their side. The government argues that 'accelerated growth (is) the most powerful instrument to redistribute opportunities'. Education is to be relied on as the principal instrument for reconciling in the future the inevitable imbalances produced by opting for permanent growth. Just as market signals have elicited growth, so runs their argument, so shall they ultimately yield higher incomes for the poor by judiciously investing in human capital. The government has not been convinced, either by its own experience or that of the other developing countries that governmental programmes which are aimed directly at alleviating rural poverty, can be successfully applied on a nation wide scale. It believes that high economic growth rates based primarily on the performance of the industrial sector offer the most likely chance of absorbing the marginal population into the modern sector.

And it is undoubtedly true that the Brazilian government has used the enormous revenues it has earned so far from taxing this economic growth to spend sizeable sums of money on schools, health and sanitary services, housing and regional development.

Public expenditure on education approached 4.5 per cent

of GNP last year, compared with 3.4 per cent in 1972. The government aim, before the year is out, to have 80 per cent school enrollment for the 5-14 age group. The national literacy campaign has already trained 3.5 million people in the first two years of its operation. The housing programme has as its goal the construction of two million units by 1980 for families with incomes of between one and three minimum wages. The water and sewerage programme has a target of bringing water supply to 80 per cent of residents and sewerage to 50 per cent.

More than this, however, is the very visible witness that the high growth rate has had great success in absorbing the new proletariat, even though it is increasing at 5.2 per cent a year. There are no small boys, homeless, sleeping on the pavements at night. Very different from the streets of Lima or Bogota. The shanty town areas in Sao Paulo have less than 4 per cent of the population — extraordinarily low by Latin American standards. And there are reports of tight urban and rural labour markets in the south, even for relatively unskilled workers.

So what does this do with the arguments of those who would scorn Brazil's way of development? Perhaps it is true, although there is no way of testing such a hypothesis yet, that an economic growth rate of 10 per cent achieves things which a 6 per cent growth rate in Pakistan and Mexico cannot. Perhaps there is a critical point — 8 per cent or 9 per cent or 9½ per cent — at which employment can be created faster or as fast as immigrants are sucked in?

Yet for all the undoubted achievements of the Brazilian phenomenon, we are left with certain questions.

Could other countries do what Brazil has done even if they wanted to? Pakistan and Mexico have tried and failed.

Is Brazil's 'success' going to continue for long? What will happen now its growth rate has dropped below 8 per cent? Will not its urban situation then get out of control like everyone else's? (And even today its 'success' does not extend much beyond Rio and Sao Paulo. In Recife, a town of over a million inhabitants, 60 per cent of the people live in favelas.)

Does not Brazil's incentive-led growth produce a mentality that works actively against development? Rio de Janeiro has more doctors per head of population than any other city in the world, yet in the Brazilian interior it has one of the world's lowest ratios.

Why should this enormous investment in education necessarily produce more equality? Education as practised in Brazil and most other developing countries too often encourages young people to leave the land and become part of the depressed urban proletariat. (Whereas if education was linked with agricultural knowledge and land reform, it could become a great liberating force.)

Is it not true that none of the social programmes that are much discussed — housing, education, sanitary services — will reach the really poor? Is not their aim rather to help create a stable upper working class?

Won't the increasing inequality of incomes produce enormous political stresses that will one day tear the fabric of the country apart and set growth of any kind back for years?

One final question is this: is there not a more human way of achieving economic development? One fraught with such inequalities as the Brazilian/Mexican/Pakistani way does not leave much room for the poor to have a say in their own destiny. And is not that what development is all about — in the end?

All the evidence suggests that the escape route from poverty that leads through the city and the industrial sector is fraught with many more difficulties than was thought likely when newly independent countries started on this path a decade or two ago. It is deeply ironic that both the major schools of economic thought — capitalist and socialist — preached similar false solutions. Many socialists argued that real independence was impossible without a strong industrial base and the West often argued that a developing industrial sector was the most effective way of attracting outside capital.

The Third World countries are now landed with the results of this mistaken advice — chronic food shortages, a demoralised countryside, a fast expanding urban slum population and a growing inequality of incomes.

Some developing countries have only one or two of these problems; some have them all. But the world over there is a growing awareness that all is not well and that the time has come to look for an alternative development strategy.

Could it be that one way of resolving simultaneously the inter-
locked problems of food shortages, overpopulation, migration,
slum creation and income distribution would be to give greater
emphasis to developing the countryside — not the countryside
of the landowners, the estate, the latifundia, but that of the
small independent farmer? Already we know enough about
agricultural technique to get the smallholder to raise his
productivity so that by 1985 his yields would be increasing
at 5 per cent a year. And if this were done it would
certainly break the back of the immediate crisis, even if it
did not solve the problem of poverty.

Quite clearly, however, this is not just a technical problem
but one that throws into question the whole social and
political direction of an economy. But before we come to
these more subtle questions we should examine the problem
in its more technical components.

Most developing countries lie within the zone of tropical
climatic conditions. Although there is no generalised tropical
climate, the characteristics of fairly equable high temperatures
and irregular rainfall regimes occur throughout the area.
Three broad climatic regions can be distinguished. First there
are the equatorial lowlands where there is no true dry season.
Temperatures are consistently high and the annual rainfall
average is about sixty inches, although it does not fall
uniformly throughout the year. Brazil and West Africa are
two regions which fall within the equatorial lowland category.
The second important climatic area is that of the tropical
monsoon, as typified in South Asia. In this climatic region
there is a marked seasonality of rainfall. These two regions
make up about 10 per cent of the earth's land surface.
Finally there is the tropical savannah region, which alone
covers over 10 per cent of the earth's land surface. Annual

average rainfall is only twenty-four inches, concentrated in one or more parts of the year, and there is at least one dry season. Vast areas of Africa and Latin America experience savannah climate.

The impression we tend to have of the tropics is one of luxuriant vegetation and fertile, productive soils. This is not so at all. Tropical climates have several serious disadvantages for agriculture.

First, humidity is the most important factor in tropical climates, as it is humidity, not temperature, that governs rainfall and evaporation. Many parts of the tropics suffer either from continuous rainfall, which encourages dense impassable vegetation, or from heavy seasonal storms, which cause rapid water run-off and loss of the top soil layer. Rainfall intensity in Africa can be anything up to four inches an hour.

The greatest drawback is the unreliability of rainfall. Often when rainfall is seasonal it does not arrive when it is needed and as a result either planting is delayed and the growth cycle upset or young seedlings wither away for lack of moisture. The high temperatures cause rapid evaporation of water, and so storage of excess water in the wet season to be utilised in the dry season is a difficult and expensive problem.

Secondly, nearly all developing countries that are not in high mountainous areas experience continuous and intensive heat. Heat encourages the spread of disease, especially where the humidity is high. It severely reduces the pace of human and animal activity. Soil fertility is also seriously impaired: temperature affects the solubility of the soil's nutrients and the desiccation and loss of organic matter from the soil. In the Congo it has been estimated that a rise in temperature of 1 degree Fahrenheit over 97 degrees Fahrenheit causes a loss of twenty-five pounds of nitrogen per acre and unprotected soils lose one thousand pounds of nitrogen per acre — an enormous amount.

Thirdly in the tropics there is a continual struggle between conservation and degradation of soil resources. Chemical reactions such as oxidisation take place at between two to four times their speed in temperature lands. The breakdown of leaf litter and plant debris by insects, fungi, bacteria and other organisms is so rapid that one rarely finds undecomposed plant matter on the surface. Humus, the organic matter which is formed by the breakdown of the plant and animal residues of the soil, does not form easily in these conditions and only makes up some 3 to 4 per cent of the soil content. Humus is an important source of nitrogen, phosphorus and sulphur. It also binds the soil together and gives it its texture and substance. Without humus in the soil, nutrients are easily leached far below the reach of the roots of most cultivated plants.

Leaching is a very serious problem in the tropics. The heavy showers falling on poorly structured soils cause a downward movement of water in the soil. With it silica and soil nutrients are leached and aluminium and iron remain near the surface. In forested areas the nutrients are brought back to the surface again by the deep roots. Also when the leaves fall, or the tree dies, nutrients are returned to the soil. The danger to the soil comes when the forest is cleared under pressure of population. Vast areas of land can then easily be laid to a sterile waste because the natural cycle is interrupted. The soils associated with leaching are called laterite soils.

Not all soils are infertile, however. Where the texture of the soil is good, e.g. in loam soils, then they do not provide a serious limitation to agriculture, so long as they are not misused. In fact it is often irrelevant to compare the nutrient content of temperate and tropical soils, since many tropical crops either do not require some nutrients, for instance calcium, or have become adapted to the deficiencies. In other words the soil potential is not always as low as one might imagine.

Soil erosion by water is also problematic in the tropics. When the sparse vegetation cover is removed, then heavy storms can easily wash away the light friable soils, often eroding great gulleys and carrying the top soil into rivers and out to sea. Literally millions of acres of cropland in Asia, Africa, the Middle East and the Andean countries are being abandoned each year because severe soil erosion has made them unproductive.

Fourthly, most of the diseases of temperate lands are rife in the developing countries, whilst many of these countries suffer also from certain endemic and epidemic diseases which are brought about because of the extreme climate.

Malaria is the most widespread of these non-European diseases. It severely weakens those it attacks: the bouts of fever sap a man's physical strength and make him unfit for any kind of sustained effort. Hence agriculture does not receive all the care it needs and the food supply is reduced. In this way a vicious circle is formed. Weakened by insufficient nourishment, the body offers little resistance to infection. Weakened by disease, a man cannot provide the effort required to produce an adequate supply of food, and so it goes on. Before 1955, when the WHO launched a massive malarial eradication programme, it was estimated that 63 per cent of the world's population (excluding China) lived in malaria-infested regions. Now the percentage is sixteen.

Intestinal diseases, contracted by eating raw foodstuffs, drinking water or just walking in bare feet (the larvae penetrate through the skin), are common in most poor countries, as are many other debilitating diseases.

In marked contrast, the life of pioneers clearing the wastes of Siberia, Canada and New South Wales in the eighteenth and nineteenth centuries was rough but healthy. On today's frontiers of development, however, disease takes a heavy toll, both in life and energy. Progress, therefore is necessarily slow and painful. But, you may say, is not Washington for example built on what was a disease-ridden swamp and does it not suffer from a hot and humid climate as unpleasant as many developing countries? Yes, indeed. But it was made habitable by techniques and energy brought from more moderate climes. Without that outside help the environment in the developing world can be too overpowering for man to cope.

The agricultural systems in the tropics, notably shifting cultivation and wet rice farming, are well adapted to the prevailing environment. In shifting cultivation a piece of land is farmed for a year or two and then left fallow for twenty years or more. It then reverts to its original bush covering in order to restore the nutrients to the soil, ready to be used again for cultivation. However with increasing population density this system of cultivation has come under a great deal of pressure. Fallow periods are shortened and the soil is overcultivated and becomes exhausted. In parts of Africa there is still land available at the margins of cultivation which can be utilised by the expanding number of shifting cultivators. But in other parts of the tropics, the system cannot carry a heavier burden of population and there is no spare land to bring into cultivation. It is in these areas that alternative farming methods must be developed in order to restore the man/land balance and provide the necessary food.

The rice-growing regions are the major exception to this pattern. Here, because of rice's unique yielding capacity and because of the large river valleys in Asia, such as the Yangtze and the Ganges, which flood periodically, bringing down rich silt from the volcanic mountains in the interior, there are agricultural systems that support huge stable populations of great density. Rice moreover is a crop which requires very few nutrients and survives well on tropical soils without needing artificial fertilisers. Since rice areas are permanently flooded there is no soil erosion problem. There is also no need for fallow periods.

The other exception to the pattern of shifting cultivation is found in some of the mountainous areas of the developing countries: places like the White Highlands of Kenya, the Adamoua Massif of the Cameroons and the innermost basins of many South American countries. They have the advantage of a temperate climate and in many cases volcanic soils which are extremely rich in plant nutrients.

Without any interference from man, the tropical environment is not on the whole conducive to high agricultural productivity. Yet, given control of the water supply, eradication of disease and improvements of farming techniques, there is potential for much greater productivity. It is important not to overlook a number of advantages inherent in tropical climates. There can be plant growth all year round. The tropics thus have a great natural potential for multiple cropping, though this is again limited by the lack of available water throughout the year. Multiple cropping would make much more intensive use of existing cultivated areas. Already in China nearly half the cultivated land is said to be under two crops per year. In India the figure is less than 18 per cent.

In addition most tropical areas do have a sufficient annual water supply, although distributed unevenly through the year. Agriculture would be more productive if water could be stored and supply ensured in the dry seasons. At present, where irrigation is not available, only one crop can be grown during the wet season. With controlled water supply another crop, perhaps a drought-resistant one, like sorghum or millet, could be grown in the dry season.

There is much room for research into such drought-resistant crops or into shortening the growing period of existing crops. Commercial use could be made of native flora and fauna, rather than introducing non-indigenous crops or livestock which have little resistance to drought or disease. Productivity can be increased if the drawbacks of the environment are overcome — certainly not an impossible task — and the optimum use made of the main climatic advantage, the facility for year-round plant growth.

Despite all the problems confronting Third World agriculture, the fact is that a number of countries have shown that it is possible to keep food production well ahead of population growth.

Population in the underdeveloped countries is growing at 2.7 per cent a year, but over the twenty-year period 1952 to 1972 food production expanded at an annual rate of 6.1 per cent in Venezuela, 5.4 per cent in Togo, 5.8 per cent in Lebanon and 5.3 per cent in Thailand. Seven other countries topped the 5 per cent mark: Bolivia, Costa Rica, Cyprus, Ecuador, Malaysia, Libya and Mexico. Regrettably, however, many of the countries have not followed the strategy we will advocate in this chapter — of emphasising the potential productivity of small farmers. In the north-east of Thailand the poorest half of the farmers during the 1960s saw their average income decline, from about half the region's average to less than 20 per cent. The average income of half the rural households suffered a negative growth rate both in the northeast and the south.[1] In Mexico 80 per cent of the increase in production between 1950 and 1960 came from only 3 per cent of the farms. The number of landless rural labourers increased from 2.3 million to 3.3 million. Because of labour-displacing mechanisation, the number of days worked by each labourer declined by almost a half from 194 to 100. The already low incomes of these workers actually declined from sixty-eight to fifty-six dollars a year during the decade, at a time when per capita income for Mexico as a whole increased from 308 to 405 dollars.[2]

In both these cases people were pushed off the land and into the shanty towns, and in the next chapter — on the Green Revolution — we will examine these problems in more detail. In this chapter we argue that if certain bottlenecks in the production system were removed, 5 per cent growth rates in agriculture could be achieved without these harmful consequences; and that the 5 per cent growth could be based on the production potential of the peasant farmers. These bottlenecks are archaic land tenure arrangements, lack of credit, poor research and extension services, unproductive agricultural techniques, shortages of fertiliser and water supply and an underdeveloped rural-industrial sector.

Table 15 shows dramatically the number of people held on the land by a range of different countries. Those at the top of the league, Taiwan, Japan, South Korea and Egypt, are those who have had vigorous land reform and have emphasised, as the backbone of their highly successful economic development, the role of the small peasant farmer. Those at the bottom (apart from the United States) are dominated by landlord-sharecropper arrangements with the tenant supplying up to half his production as rent.

Farms in Taiwan have yields per acre six times higher than the Philippines or India. In Taiwan in 1950 agricultural employment was seventeen million. Since then it has increased at 1.2 per cent a year. In 1968 it increased by 2.1 per cent.

Table 15: Agricultural workers per 100 acres 1965

Country	Number of workers per 100 acres
Japan	87
Taiwan	75
India	36
South Korea	79
Philippines	29
Ceylon	49
Colombia	20
Brazil	17
Mexico	12
Egypt	71
Israel	11
Yugoslavia	29
Morocco	10
USA	less than 2

Source: Derived from tables in FAO Production Yearbook 1969

We would note that it is likely — if statistics were forthcoming — that China would also be near the top of this table (see chapter 9 for an evaluation of the Chinese agricultural system).

But for all the evidence that small-scale farmers are the most productive, many if not most countries assume the opposite is the case. The Brazilians, for example, argue — and they have in their north-east regions the most serious maldistribution of land in the world — that realism calls for caution in land reform. It is the bigger farmers, they say, who will more readily respond to the availability of credit and new technological ideas. Yet it has been shown in Brazil that returns to scale for different size farms (assuming the same quality of land) is relatively constant. In other words, given the same level of inputs, small farmers are as efficient as large farmers. Moreover, it has also been established (and an institution no less conservative than the World Bank has accepted these findings) that the intensity of land use declines as farm size rises.[3] This suggests that a distribution of land from large farmers to small would increase land utilisation and consequently agricultural production. Studies in other parts of the world have confirmed these Brazilian observations.

Theoretically the effects of land reform on agrarian productivity could best be judged if output in a given year could be compared before and after reform. Unfortunately this is not possible as there is no situation where change has taken place and only one variable — the size of farm — has altered. The best we can do is to compare the productivity of groups of different size farms.

The World Bank and the FAO have made two such studies. They both found independently that a smaller average size of holding and a low concentration of ownership produced an increase in output per hectare. The World Bank study was of forty-one countries and the findings are produced in table 16.

Similar findings have been made in cross-sectional studies in a number of individual countries. In Sri Lanka, in 1966-67, the yield of paddy was found to be higher on the smaller farms than on the larger: 36/37 bushels per acre on farms of less than one acre and 33/34 on those of more. In Central Thailand yields were 304 kilos/*rai* on holdings of two to six acres but down to 194 kilos/*rai* on holdings of six acres or more. Small farms in the Philippines with less than two

Table 16: Productivity, employment and the distribution of land in different countries

Country	Data year	Farm GDP per hectare (US$)	Farm GDP per worker (US$)	Employment per hectare	Average holding size (hectare)	Gini's index of land con- centration
EUROPE						
Greece	1961	424	848	0.50	3.18	.597
Spain	1962	90	980	0.09	14.85	.832
CENTRAL AMERICA						
Costa Rica	1963	83	951	0.09	40.74	
Dominican Republic	1971	129	463	0.28	8.64	
El Salvador	1961	186	489	0.38	6.95	
Guatemala	1964	144	492	0.29	8.17	
Mexico	1960	22	569	0.04	123.9	
Nicaragua	1963	55	580	0.09	37.34	
SOUTH AMERICA						
Argentina	1970	18	1903	0.01	270.1	.873
Brazil	1960	14	285	0.05	79.25	.845
Chile	1965	18	692	0.03	118.5	

Table 16 (continued)

Country	Data year	Farm GDP per hectare (US$)	Farm GDP per worker (US$)	Employment per hectare	Average holding size (hectare)	Gini's index of land con- centration
SOUTH AMERICA (continued)						
Colombia	1960	67	663	0.10	22.60	.865
Paraguay	1961	11	479	0.02	108.7	
Peru	1961	50	477	0.10	20.37	.947
Uruguay	1966	14	1333	0.01	208.8	.833
Venezuela	1961	31	925	0.03	81.24	.936
ASIA						
India	1960	172	141	1.22	6.52	.607
Indonesia	1963	323	149	2.17	1.05	
Iran	1960	187	581	0.32	6.05	.624
Korea, Republic of	1970	1085	377	2.88	0.85	
Japan	1960	1720	1188	1.45	1.18	.473
Nepal	1961/62	352	138	2.54	1.23	
Pakistan	1960	240	249	0.96	2.35	.607
Philippines	1960	250	200	1.25	3.59	.580

Table 16 (continued)

Country	Data year	Farm GDP per hectare (US$)	Farm GDP per worker (US$)	Employment per hectare	Average holding size (hectare)	Gini's index of land con-centration
ASIA (continued)						
Sri Lanka	1962	376	337	1.12	1.61	
Taiwan	1960/61	841	410	2.05	1.27	.474
Thailand	1963	166	137	1.21	3.47	
Turkey	1963	155	243	0.64	5.03	.611
Vietnam, Republic of	1960	355	127	2.79	1.33	
AFRICA						
Botswana	1969/70	168	142	1.18	4.75	
Kenya	1969	183	140	1.31	871.3	
Malagasy	1961/62	293	88	3.32	1.04	
Mali	1960	98	48	2.06	4.35	
Morocco	1961	144	295	0.49	4.62	
Senegal	1960	209	174	1.20	3.62	
Tanzania	1960	485	94	5.16	785.7	
Togo	1961/62	189	180	1.05	2.62	

Table 16 (continued)

Country	Data year	Farm GDP per hectare (US$)	Farm GDP per worker (US$)	Employment per hectare	Average holding size (hectare)	Gini's index of land con-centration
AFRICA (continued)						
Tunisia	1961/62	42	341	0.12	15.41	
United Arab Republic	1960/61	681	360	1.89	1.59	.748
Uganda	1963/64	167	198	0.84	3.29	
Zambia	1960	68	101	0.67	11.73	

Sources: Cols. 1 and 3 are based on FAO Production Yearbook, 1971, pp. 10-11, 21-23, and col. 4 on UN, *Monthly Bulletin of Statistics*, XXVI, no. 4, April 1972 and XXVII, no. 11, November 1973. For currency exchange rates, IMF, *International Financial Statistics*, XXVI, no. 8, August 1973. GDP in agriculture shown here includes, unless otherwise indicated, agriculture, hunting, forestry and fishing.

hectares produced 2.9 tons of paddy per hectare. Those over four hectares produced only 2.2 tons.

The main reason behind the higher productivity per acre on small farms is that the inputs are greater. A smallholder makes a more intensive use of factors of production, such as labour, draught animals, water supply and even mechanisation per unit area of his fields than a farmer cultivating more extensive areas. For instance in Thailand, there is one buffalo for every 4 *rais* on farms between 2 and 6 *rais* (1 *rai* = 0.3 acres). But on farms of over 140 *rais* there is only one buffalo for every 30 *rais*.[4] The larger farms have several drawbacks, such as the lack of natural fertiliser to cover extensive areas and a greater proportion of marginal land included in the cultivated area.

Table 17 gives the results of a systematic analysis of the difference between large 'multifamily' farms and small 'subfamily' farms in Argentina, Brazil, Chile, Colombia, Ecuador and Guatemala. Output per hectare was found to be three to fourteen times greater on average on the smaller farms than on the larger ones.

The significance of these findings cannot be overestimated. For years the defenders of the *status quo* have argued that land reform will end up by creating a depressed peasantry, too ignorant and small-minded to apply the knowledge that is necessary if productivity is to be increased. This view does not stand up to close scrutiny. The fact is that there are negative economies of scale in most farm production. Small-holdings incur the lowest production costs, by using family labour and making intensive use of other inputs, while also producing more output per acre. In India the value of output per acre on farms between nought and five acreas was 200 Rupees in 1969. On farms of twenty to fifty acres the value was only 154 Rupees per acre.[5] Large-scale farms aim to maximise profits by using hired labour until incremental production covers incremental costs. This is usually less than the output per acre that would be produced if the object were to maximise output.

The negative economies of scale are even more apparent when the social costs of underutilisation of land and labour

Table 17: Agricultural output per hectare and per worker by farm size, Latin America

Country	Year	1 Smallest sub family farms	2 Largest multifamily farms	3 Ratio Col. 1 to Col. 2
(National Monetary Unit per Agricultural hectare)				
Argentina	1960	2492	304	8.2
Brazil	1950	1498	170	8.8
Chile	1955	334	41	8.2
Colombia	1960	1198	84	14.3
Ecuador	1954	1862	660	2.8
Guatemala	1950	63	16	3.9
(National Monetary Unit per worker)				
Argentina	1960	40	192	.21
Brazil	1950	1197	8237	.14
Chile	1955	268	1171	.23
Colombia	1960	972	9673	.10
Guatemala	1950	74	523	.14

Source: Barraclough and Collarte (1973), Table B-2

are taken into account. Since there is a negative correlation between farm size and productivity and a positive relationship between labour input and yield, land reform becomes a key issue in the effort to increase output and employment.

However there are still some worrying criticisms of the land reform school of thought that have to be answered. It is said by the critics that a reduction in land concentration could — at least in the short run — lead to a shortfall in the amount farmers produce for market. And a study carried out in India, to take one example, shows that small farmers sell only 24.5 per cent of their output whereas the larger farms sell 65.4 per cent.

However the mistake has been to look at the ratio of production surplus rather than at the changes in total output. Since per acre yields on small farms can be higher than on large farms total output can increase to more than compensate for the rise in individual consumption ratios. Besides, the lower ratio of production surplus has its positive side. It means that the poorer families are eating more themselves. Not only is this good in itself, but over time it is likely to increase their productivity. It should not be forgotten too that if land reform did not take place it is likely that many of the peasants would move to the town. There they would have to be fed by the bigger farmers using imported capital-intensive equipment and consuming imported luxury goods. Small farmers producing their own food make for less pressure on the balance of payments.

Another objection to land redistribution is said to be the negative impact it would have on the savings rate. Savings are a key issue in development. Without savings, either private or state, there can be no investment. And without investment there can be no growth in productive capacity.

There is, as it happens, little evidence of what happens to savings under the impact of land reform. But common sense would suggest that savings rates will perform rather like the marketable surplus. So we will see some small farmers becoming net 'dissavers' — perhaps because they run down existing soil fertility, whereas large farmers, although they can become 'dissaver' too (by, say, using their capital for

Table 18: Tenancy and sharecropping in selected countries[1]

Country	Renting and sharecropping as per cent of total		Number of renters and sharecroppers[2] '000
	Number of farms[2]	Farmland %	
ASIA			
India	27.3	n.a.	13,350
Indonesia	35.9	25.9	4,392
Malaya, Federation of	31.2	15.7	141
Pakistan[3]	43.4	57.0	5,271
Philippines	54.3	40.4	1,176
Vietnam, Republic of	<u>70.3</u>	<u>70.0</u>	<u>1,334</u>
Total	33.0	45.7[4]	25,664
NEAR EAST AND NORTH AFRICA			
Iran	66.7	73.4	1,253
Tunisia	23.3	32.0	76
United Arab Republic	<u>62.1</u>	<u>57.2</u>	<u>1,020</u>
Total	61.1	62.6	2,349
LATIN AMERICA AND CARIBBEAN			
Dominican Republic	28.9	n.a.	129
Guatemala	22.4	16.6	93
Nicaragua	26.3	n.a.	27
Trinidad and Tobago	49.5	32.8	18
Chile	49.3	24.4	128
Colombia	<u>31.5</u>	<u>13.5</u>	<u>381</u>
Total	31.4	19.2[4]	776

[1] Data refer to latest available year in 1960s and therefore do not reflect land action, on the one hand, and changes in the work force on the other.

[2] Includes holdings operated under more than one tenure form (21.8 per cent).

[3] Includes both Pakistan and Bangladesh.

[4] India, Dominican Republic, and Nicaragua are excluded, due to lack of data.

Sources: *Report on the 1960 World Census of Agriculture* Vol.5, FAO, Rome, 1971, pp. 92-97

consumption), usually have a positive savings rate. A recent study in the state of Hariana, India, confirms this. Here the savings ratio was 0.24 per cent for small farmers, 8.5 per cent for medium farmers, and 1.63 per cent for large farmers. A further study in Orissa, India, underlined these results. But again, as with marketable surpluses, the shortfall in individual rates can be compensated for by an increase in aggregate rates simply because, after land reform, the countryside is running under a more productive smallholder system.

A word of caution: land reform must give the peasant farmer sufficient land to enable him to produce enough not to be a dissaver and to grow enough to have a surplus for marketable sales.

The final question we must deal with — and this one will not go away so easily — is this: in areas where land reform is most necessary is there enough land to go around? Or is it inevitable that at least some of the people must leave the land and move to the town?

In the Americas where population is not dense and yet where urban drift is extreme, land reform would enable practically all the rural population to have land. In other parts of the globe, however, the pressure of population is such that there is just not enough land to meet the minimum requirements of all the claimants. In India even if the maximum holdings were twenty acres the available land (forty-three million acres) would be barely sufficient to bring up the size of the smallest holdings to five acres. And even if this were done there would still be no land for the twenty to twenty-five million landless families. In Bangladesh a low ten-acre ceiling would not be sufficient to give every small farmer a two-acre patch. Again there would be no land for the landless. In Haiti only 3.71 acres would be available for the peasant farmer.

This does not mean we have to accept that those 'left over' must become the dispossessed residents of urban squalor. The countryside has many other possibilities beside the farm and these are examined below.

A final postscript on two things: cost and stability. Land reform is rarely expensive. It does not require large outlays

Table 19: Landless farm workers in selected countries[1]

Country	Number of landless workers '000	Landless workers as % of active population in agriculture %	Active agricultural population as % of total active population %
ASIA			
India	70,000	47	68
Indonesia	5,673	20	70
Pakistan[2]	8,013	29	70
Total	83,686	41	68
MIDDLE EAST AND NORTH AFRICA			
Iran	903	25	46
United Arab Republic	1,865	38	55
Algeria	1,099	60	56
Morocco	484	19	61
Tunisia	210	20	46
Total	4,561	33	58
LATIN AMERICA AND CARIBBEAN			
Costa Rica	122	53	45
Dominican Republic	179	25	61
Honduras	138	27	67
Jamaica	72	41	27
Mexico (1970)	2,499	49	39
Nicaragua (1971)	101	43	47
Argentina	694	51	15
Chile	378	66	28
Colombia	1,158	42	45
Ecuador	391	39	54
Peru	557	30	46
Uruguay	99	55	17
Brazil	3,237	26	44
Venezuela	287	33	26
Total	9,912		39

[1] Unless otherwise indicated, data refer to latest year available in 1960s and thus do not reflect recent reform actions, on the one hand, and changes in the work force, on the other.

[2] Includes population now belonging to Bangladesh.

Source: ILO *Year Book of Labor Statistics,* 1971, pp. 43-294 and *1972,* pp. 44-301

of government funds. Payment is usually in bonds redeemable at a future date. It has been estimated that in those Latin American countries that used nonconfiscatory reforms, only 9 to 15 per cent of the total reform-related cash budgets went for landowners' compensation. And of course, when land is confiscated as part of a revolutionary process, as it was in Mexico, Bolivia, China and Cuba, there is even less public expenditure.

Land reform however, whether by revolution or by reform, usually brings instability in its wake. Production goes down and traditional marketing and delivery systems are thrown into confusion. Yet with good management, as the World Bank has concluded, this unsettled period can be kept short and temporary.

Credit is a key element in providing the impetus that will increase the productivity of agriculture. Not only can it remove financial constraints, but it can provide the incentive to adopt technologies that otherwise would be too expensive.

Farmers have traditionally depended on credit — the credit of the money-lender or the *hacienda* owner, who all too often charge exorbitant rates of interest of 40 or more per cent. The number of farmers using institutional credit (the bank or legally recognised credit institutions) varies widely in different parts of the world. In parts of Africa only about 1 per cent of the farmers use such credit. In Taiwan, almost all do. For Africa as a whole the total is 5 per cent, for Latin America and Asia (excluding Taiwan) it is about 15 per cent.

More often than not it is the large farmers who benefit from credit. Nearly 80 per cent of the small farmers have no access to credit. Small farmers generally spend less than 20 per cent of what is needed on such inputs as improved seeds, pesticides and fertilisers because they simply do not have the resources. In Asia, for example, the cost of fertiliser and pesticides required to make the maximum use of the new high-yielding varieties of wheat and rice ranges from twenty to eighty dollars per hectare. But the small farmer cannot afford more than six dollars. And often he ends up borrowing those six dollars at usurious rates of interest.

110

The Brazilian government'a attitude to credit is fairly typical. It has in recent years been steadily increasing its credit provision for farms. Agricultural credit as a proportion of net agricultural domestic credit has increased from about 26 per cent in 1966 to over 50 per cent in 1972. Although the government took no special measures to ensure that the smaller farmers would get a fair share of this new credit the assumption was that since it was there they could simply ask for it. Agricultural loans were made cheaper than loans to other sectors of the economy, and the smaller the loan, the lower the rate of interest. But in practice there was little take-up by the small farmers and they continued by and large to rely on landowners and trading companies. A recent survey of cotton farmers in the interior state of Ceara found that only one out of sixty sharecroppers had received institutional credit. But almost all had one or more informal loans obtained from farm owners or local merchants. Sadly most of these people using credit were not using it to improve their farms but to finance the purchase of the basic necessities of life until the next harvest came in.

The Brazilian experience is an everyday one. Unfamiliarity with bank procedures (five-page forms are not uncommon), insufficient numbers of bank branches in rural areas, insecurity of tenure, high production risks and lack of profitable use for credit, all militate against the smallholder taking the initiative to seek credit out. And even if he does, banks often turn such requests down when they have a steady demand from more creditworthy customers.

This lack of credit to small farmers is a tragic misallocation. Several studies[6] in Brazil have shown that some reallocation of credit from large agricultural users to small- and medium-sized farms would have a positive impact on output and would help to achieve higher rates of employment and a better income distribution.

In the Dominican Republic a fascinating experiment is attempting to circumnavigate these barriers to credit distribution. Convinced that small farmers could make use of credit, if given proper back-up with agricultural expertise, the Dominican Development Foundation (a private non-government organisation) has tried to find a way that is non-bureaucratic, simple and above all appealing to small farmers. They have done this by working through groups of farmers rather than individuals. Farmers who want to receive credit must set up an association, receive the money in the name of the group and agree to be responsible as a group for the repayments of individual members. Banks have found that 10 per cent or more of small farmers default on their loans; the Foundation by this method has got the defaulting rate down to 4.2 per cent. The social pressure of not letting the group down works astonishingly effectively.

The groups vary enormously. Some of them are quite loosely knit with individual members farming independently and only coming together to receive the loan. In others the collective system works at nearly every level of the productive enterprise. For example: a tomato farm is worked by a group of thirty families — they share the land and the cost of the large pump to bring water up from the river. And they organise the planting, weeding and reaping operations so everyone takes an equal part of the load. This project — the community of Fondo Negro — has established itself in one of the driest and most impoverished parts of the country. The annual rainfall is only 650 mm and average monthly temperatures vary from twenty-five to thirty degrees Centigrade. Yet these peasant farmers have cultivated 115 hectares of land and have made in the first year a net profit of 263 dollars per hectare, or approximately 1,052 dollars per family. Before they were set up in business by the Foundation and given the credit to prime their operations the yearly income had been about 100 dollars a family.

Here is a detailed breakdown of the economics of the project:

The project consisted in putting under production 115 hectares of lands devoted to the cultivation of tomatoes. A yield of 546 cwt. per hectare was obtained and this produced 62,790 cwt. which was sold at US$1.50 and brought in the sum of US$94,185 in the first agricultural year.

The costs per hectare were US$577.20, the direct costs of

112

cultivation totalling US$66,378. Out of this US$4,320 were paid to the 30 agricultural workers participating as a labour force at the rate of US$2.00 per day during 24 days per month over a period of 3 months. US$62,050 were spent on other operational costs and agricultural expenses.

The capital investment reached $18,292.77 of which $3,060.00 related to enclosures and piping and $15,232.77 to irrigation equipment and plant.

There was a depreciation for this period of $1,829.28, taking 10 years as the time of use for the capital investment. Hence the direct profits from the cultivation were US$25,997.72, that is to say $225.89 per hectare. The economic surplus for the group was US$30,297.72, if we add to the profit the amount they obtained as payment for labour. This gives an average profit of $263.46 per hectare.

The Foundation's more advanced groups are now having their loan applications transferred to commercial banks. Convinced that these small farmers will not default after all, the big banks have been persuaded to take them on as normal customers. So far 105 groups are receiving loans in this way and the defaulting rate is down to 1 per cent.

All the good ideas in the world are useless unless a way can be found to get them to the small farmer. Someone who has the relevant information on improved seeds, fertiliser, rotation systems, agricultural tools, tube wells etc. must be on hand — someone who preferably lives with the village people, knows their ways and earns their trust.

But the number of such people is abysmally low. In the developed countries the ratio of government agricultural agents to farm families is about 1:400. In developing countries it averages 1:8,000 — and most of these concern themselves with the larger farmers. The projected number of trained personnel who will graduate annually from existing agricultural educational institutions will satisfy at the most optimistic estimate less than half the total needs of the Third World.

Research, too, is grossly undermanned. So much can be

achieved through research programmes that seek out varieties of seed that resist disease and produce increased yields. The potential is enormous: Soviet wheat yields are only one fourth those of corn in the United States; Chinese rice yields one third; and Indian rice yields scarcely one sixth.

Gunnar Myrdal observes of Asian agriculture:

Without any innovations and even without any investment other than longer and more efficient work, agricultural yields could be raised very substantially. This is demonstrated by the different levels of yields as between districts or even individual farms revealed by management surveys. Still greater increases in yields could be attained by applying modern scientific agricultural technology.[7]

And the new 'miracle seeds' of the Green Revolution in Asia and Latin America have doubled yields. The World Bank rural development experts argue that tropical farms using the best of modern science and seeking to maximise yield per hectare per day through multiple cropping can attain yield increases of *six* to *sixteen* times present levels.

Yet for all the potential in this kind of scientific work, a World Bank sample of five major developed and five major developing countries found a wide contrast in research spending. In the rich countries, governments were giving between 120 and 150 dollars per farm family for research: in the developing countries it was only 50 cents to 2 dollars per family.

Lurking behind these statistics of agricultural inadequacy is the educational system. They appear appallingly uniform. Whether the systems have been laid down by colonial regimes or by independent governments, agriculture is not regarded as something worth teaching at school or university. Some developing countries have a surplus of university graduates in general studies, law and the arts. In India, for example, there are now so many unemployed graduates it has become a national problem. Yet they would not consider the possibility of going to work in the villages. And it is the same for children who leave school after four years of education.

They believe that this has at least earned them the right to turn their back on 'primitive' village life. Agriculture is despised, is old fashioned. A study of a region in the Ivory Coast[8] showed graphically the situation that exists in numerous developing countries — the higher the rate of education, the faster the exodus from the land.

Table 20

Educational level	Ratio of exodus	
	Males	*Females*
Illiterate	8	11
Literate	42	55
Primary School Certificate[1]	61	75

[1] The Primary School Certificate is an examination taken after six years of primary schooling.

An increase in agricultural production on a world scale will demand enormous amounts of fertilisers and pesticide. In Holland, where four tons of grain per hectare are obtained, fertilisers use an average 360 kilogrammes per hectare. Holland uses the same quantity of fertiliser as the whole of Latin America. Japan now uses more fertiliser than India although her cultivated area is a mere 4 per cent of India's.

The distinguished chemical engineer, Raymond Ewell, has warned us that fertiliser production, at the moment experiencing short-term difficulties, is likely to run into even more problems. In 1974 India had a million tons of fertiliser less than in 1973 which meant a drop of eight to ten million tons in the production of wheat and rice. The FAO estimated that fertiliser shortfall in the developing countries for the crop year beginning July 1974 to be two million tons. This meant a loss in grain production of about twenty million tons — enough to feed a hundred million people. The cumulative losses in fertiliser inputs in 1974 and 1975 could mean a total fall in grain production of some thirty-six million tons.

The main factor in the shortage of fertilisers available to developing countries has been the escalation of prices. Between 1973 and 1974 the price of fertilisers doubled or trebled as a result of the inflation of oil and mineral prices. The developed countries can bear the burden of higher prices and they continue to spread fertilisers lavishly over their farms, gardens and golf courses, while the supply to needy customers in the Third World is not available in the necessary quantities.

The problem of supply has been exacerbated by other forces. In 1974 the United States government released its fertiliser industry from price constraints on the condition that it provided a larger proportion of total output for the home market. The agricultural land taken out of production in the 1960s because excess output of grain was causing a collapse of prices has now been released from the land bank. A massive input of fertilisers will be needed to farm these new areas and so still less will be available for export to the non-fertiliser producing countries.

Not only are there difficulties in obtaining the fertiliser required, but there are growing problems in using it. The run-off of chemical fertiliser from farmlands into rivers and lakes leads to eutrophication or overfertilisation of fresh-water bodies. Nitrates and phosphates introduced into fresh water through run-off serve as nutrients for algae and other aquatic plant life. The algae begin to multiply in enormous profusion. Then they die and decompose. This absorbs the oxygen supply in the lake at a fast rate. Soon fish begin to die and eventually the lake will turn into a putrid and smelly swamp.

Nitrates also cause the chemical pollution of drinking water. Excessive nitrates can cause metahemoylobanemi — a physiological disorder affecting the blood's oxygen-carrying capacity. After a number of outbreaks of this disease in the early seventies in California some communities began using bottled water.

However, it is important not to over-exaggerate this danger. British experience is relevant. Britain is one of the most highly fertilised farming systems in the world, next only to Japan and the Netherlands. British farmers use three times as much fertiliser as their American counterparts. However the Royal Commisson on Environmental Pollution not long ago reported that in conditions of good husbandry run-off is not a major problem. It is clear that the developing countries are some way off having to worry about eutrophication.

It is estimated that the presently irrigated areas of the developing world — eighty-five million hectares — can be expanded by another nine million hectares. But the additional cost would be high: over 130 million dollars.[9]

In the 1950s and 1960s there was a great surge in the building of huge irrigation projects in several developing countries. Many of the world's largest rivers, such as the Yellow, Nile and Indus, were dammed and prestigious schemes started which were intended to irrigate millions of acres of farmland. However the results have not always proved successful.

The Indian government undertook several large projects between 1951 and 1965 which were supposed to cover an area of thirteen million hectares. By 1966 only a quarter of this area was actually receiving a constant supply of water. Large-scale projects have many environmental drawbacks. Water is distributed from the central reservoir to farmlands by means of canals. Up to 40 per cent of this water is then lost as a result of seepage and evaporation. If the canals are not looked after they tend to cause waterlogging and salinity develops because of high evaporation. In Pakistan it is estimated that forty thousand hectares go out of production each year because of these problems.

In cost/benefit terms the large schemes are not the most worthy of investment. It is the small projects which can make a more efficient use of the available water. These low-level technological systems can be afforded by far more farmers and benefit areas which are not as geographically localised as the large river-basin irrigation schemes.

Groundwater resources hold a great potential supply. Water is stored naturally and there is little evaporation loss. Groundwater can be tapped by hand-built wells or by tube-wells and can also be pumped to the surface by pumps drawn by animals or powered by wind or water. As each well serves a small area there is little loss of water. Throughout India and Pakistan there are hundreds of thousands of tube-wells. For every five thousand tube-wells in Pakistan one million acre feet have been added to the yearly supply of water. However many of these wells are privately built and are used by the rich farmers. There is a strong case for even smaller tube-wells made of bamboo, so that the poorest farmers can realise the benefits of irrigation.

Small, low-cost schemes provide a quick return on investment, while large projects require the outlay of vast sums of money (often borrowed from abroad at high interest rates) which only see returns on the investment some ten years later.

When we discussed land reform we pointed out that even the most equitable scheme could not give land when it was not there; that in India, for example, there would still be twenty to twenty-five million landless farmers.

A vibrant rural economy can, however, if the right structures are created, become a breeding ground for supportive economic activity. For a start seeds, tools, fertiliser and credit are needed and their provision and distribution create local jobs. And as agricultural production increases so must the processing facilities.

As farmers increase their production they also increase their purchasing power. Many, if not all, of their needs can be supplied by small-scale labour-intensive local industry. In the Pakistani Punjab, for example, where the demand for tube-wells and grain mills has grown exceedingly fast as new agricultural ideas have taken hold, the small country towns have grown into centres for the manufacture of diesel engines. There are now a hundred small engine-producing factories in the town of Dasca alone. (Unfortunately these small group manufacturers pay twice as much for some of their raw materials as larger firms because they are not big enough to qualify for an import licence that would enable them to buy imported pig iron at special prices.)

Schumacher has defined this as 'intermediate technology', that is as something between the very old and the very new. He puts it this way:

> If we define the level of technology in terms of 'equipment cost per workplace' we can call the indigenous technology (symbolically speaking) a £1 technology while that of the modern west could be called a £1000 technology. The current attempt of the developing countries, supported by foreign aid, to infiltrate the £1000 technology into their economies inevitably kills off the £1 technology at an alarming rate, destroying traditional workplaces at a much faster rate than modern workplaces can be created. . . . The average annual income per worker and the average capital per workplace in the developed countries appear to stand in a relationship of roughly 1:1. This implies, in general terms, that it takes one man one year to create one work place, or that a man would have to save one month's earnings a year for twelve years to be able to buy his own workplace. If the relationship were 1:10, it would require ten man years to create one workplace, or a man would have to save a month's earnings for 120 years before he could make himself independent. This of course is an improbability, and it follows that the £1000 technology transplanted into a country the bulk of which is stuck on the £1 technology simply cannot spread by any process of normal growth. . . . Its 'demonstration effect' is wholly negative. The vast majority of people, to whom the £1000 technology is wholly inaccessible, simply 'give up'. An appropriate technology, on the other hand, would be one which would be 'vastly superior' in productivity to their traditional technology (in its present state of decay) while at the same time being vastly cheaper and simpler than the highly sophisticated and enormously capital intensive technology of the West. As a general guide it may be said that this 'intermediate technology' should

119

be on the level of £70 – £100 equipment cost per average workplace. At this level it would stand in a tolerably realistic relationship to the annual income obtainable by an able worker outside the westernized sectors.

It is also possible to scale down some of the excesses of imported technology. Take the case of the production of plywood in Korea. What at first appears to be a manufacturing process bearing great similarities to that carried out in the rich West turns out on inspection to be full of innovative and indigenous variations. In America mechanical sensors are used to detect defects in pieces of timber, and the entire slab is then discarded. In Japan defects are discovered and then cut out by hand. In Korea, the defective area is located and then patched up by hand.

Small-scale industries need to be established in the agricultural areas to utilise rural supply for rural consumption. Agro-industries are extremely underdeveloped in the Third World and the potential rural consumer market has yet to be tapped. As the market is relatively self-contained, there is no need for a complex marketing system or highly developed infrastructure. But where industry has been decentralised just for the sake of it, as has often been the case in India, it is very inefficient since it fails to integrate with the rural hinterland.

Some economists argue that although intermediate technology optimises the ratio of output to fixed capital, it does not create a sufficient rate of surplus for reinvestment in new jobs to take place. In other words if a more expensive technology is adopted, the initial cost is high but the output is much greater, so that within a few years it has paid off the initial costs and is making substantial profits.[10] But studies made in India, Pakistan, Indonesia, Taiwan, Egypt, Chile, Mexico, Colombia, Ghana and Ethiopia show that in many types of economic enterprise small units make more effective use of the factors of production than large ones, at least in the early stages of development.

The Taiwan study, which compared small industries with an investment of under 25,000 dollars with those having an

120

investment of over 25 million dollars, showed that each additional dollar invested in the small plants created twice as much output as an additional dollar investment in the larger. Moreover it showed that labour's share of income in the small plants was double that of the large ones.[11]

Taiwan herself has followed a policy of keeping as much development in the villages and small towns as possible. In the early 1960s only 34 per cent of Taiwan's industrial employment was in the capital and regional cities, where 22 per cent of its total population lived. Under roughly comparable circumstances Colombia had 75 per cent of its industrial employment in its regional cities.[12]

Even in Switzerland, Europe's second most developed country (in terms of GNP per head), only 35 per cent of the people live in large towns. Industry has been integrated into the villages producing high-quality manufactured goods that depend not on the economies of scale but the economics of skill — and perhaps also the economics of producing without a large supervisory bureacracy.

So what is needed are small towns — small regional growth centres that act as upstream dams stemming the flow of

---

Table 21: Investment cost of increasing production and labour's share of income, by factory size, Taiwan 1961

Size of industry by amount of investment	Investment cost of increasing output by $1.00	Labour's share of income per $1.00
less than $2,500	$1.97	74¢
$2,500 – 25,000	2.52	72
25,000 – 250,000	3.26	50
250,000 – $2.5 million	3.66	39
more than $25 million	4.46	31

Source: Hsieh and Lee, *Agriculture Development in Taiwan*, p.97

---

surplus labour to the big, impersonal and overweighted metropolises. Barbara Ward has called these small centres 'counter magnets to megalopolis'. In Kumasi, for example, the Ghana Technological Development Group has been commissioned to built two hundred soap factories in various small growth centres, instead of one large factory in the capital. Once a soap factory has been built then related and supporting industries will spring up, to use for instance the by-products of soap manufacture, or a repair shop.

There are unlimited possibilities for employment in the countryside itself: digging ditches, canals, building dams, houses and roads. Yet all too often machine-oriented bureaucrats believe a bulldozer or earth-remover can do the job better. Lesotho, which has the worst soil erosion problem in the world together with an appallingly high outflow of its young men to the South African mines, had all its valleys contoured (as an anti-erosion device) by giant Australian machines. Yet the job could just as easily have been done by hand and as cheaply.

The classical economist's arguments against small-scale technologies tend to ignore some of the basic premises of intermediate technology. Maximising rural development is not just a question of increasing output. Rather, it encompasses a whole range of socio-economic factors, such as the maintenance of the structure and dignity of rural communities. Intermediate technology cannot be assessed purely in technical or economic terms: it is also a question of politics — the politics of choosing an alternative model of development from the inherited western one.

It can be done: people can be held on the land; urbanisation can be stopped in its mad rush to disaster; agricultural production can feed everyone. However it is going to cost money. One estimate[13] reckons that the annual cost of on-farm investment, land and water resource development, additional training facilities and minimum capital requirements at twenty to twenty-five billion dollars by 1985. This would be the equivalent to about 3 to 5 per cent of the combined annual GNP of the Third World.

122

Some of the resources are waiting to be tapped in the developing countries themselves: from the farmers who can generate additional saving once their escalator of growth begins to move; and from the exchequers of the central governments who so often misallocate their resources. But some — a good proportion — must come from the rich countries.

But it is also going to require political will — and political will of the kind that favours the poor, the underprivileged and the unspectacular. This is in short supply.

In this chapter we have concentrated on the technological and administrative changes that have to be made. But this is an enormous deficiency. It assumes that the present political structures favour the liberation of the poor farmers and that all that needs to be done is to present a coherent programme like the one given above. In reality all is not so simple. Too many have a vested interest in the present order for changes of this magnitude to be introduced easily. It is not uncommon, for example, to find landlords sitting in powerful positions in the legislature or occupying key government posts.

Moreover, western private investment too often works to the disadvantage of the poor: it helps with its capital intensive techniques to build up a small yet powerful privileged urban minority — both working- and middle-class — that pressures the government to concentrate its resource on the town.

In short, it is unlikely that governments are going to change of their own accord. Intellectual persuasion by World Bank experts or by Gunnar Myrdal-type studies stands little chance of having much impact. And even if it does, it is unlikely that governments, which are big-city, big-salary, big-car-centred, have the sensitivity that is necessary to deal with problems at this level.

Real rural development is only going to work when farmers' movements are given the power and resources to shape their own destiny. There are many of these dotted around the Third World (and we look at some of them in a later chapter) and they need to be encouraged and sustained. When pressure of this kind begins to build up from below and has the power that comes through unity and organisation, then, and only then, will governments begin to take notice. If at that point pressure from outside is combined with pressure from below, there is a chance that instead of such movements being repressed they will be listened to and given the resource to get on with the job.

Euphoric terms such as 'miracle rice', 'miracle wheat' and 'Green Revolution' accompanied the development of new types of grain seeds in the second half of the 1960s. The solution to the world food problem seemed at long last to be within grasping distance. And there were even doubts as to whether the markets would be able to absorb the larger amounts of cereals without massive price falls. But in 1973 the Green Revolution was declared 'dead'.[1] the bad harvest year of 1973/74 was not the only reason. This merely proved that the Green Revolution like all other agricultural activities is also dependent on the weather. More important was the dawning realisation that higher productive capacity cannot be a substitute for social change.

The expression Green Revolution was used for the first time by William S. Gaud, former Director of USAID, in March 1968 in a speech to the Society of International Development. We use the term here to mean the introduction of new high-yielding varieties (HYV) and the technological and socio-economic changes in agriculture which it has produced.

HYV are in no way miracle products. They are the results of scientific research at the Mexican International Wheat and Maize Improvement Centre (CIMMYT) and the International Rice Research Institute (IRRI) in the Philippines.

These are part of a whole network of research centres which are concerned with the development of new varieties of seed in different parts of the world. For instance the International Institute of Tropical Agriculture (IITA) in Nigeria researches into the problems of agriculture in the humid tropics, the International Centre of Tropical Agriculture (CIAT) in Colombia studies agriculture in the low-latitude tropics and the International Crops Research Institute of the Semi-Arid Tropics (ICRISAT) in Hyderabad,

125

India, researches into agricultural and water-conservation methods for small farmers in hot, dry regions. Research programmes for the improvement of varieties such as oats, sorghum, cassava, pulses and soya bean are being carried out, as well as for the better known varieties, such as wheat, rice and maize.

The new varieties are the result of countless crossings of local varieties which exhibit greatly differing genetic characteristics. Their main characteristics are as follows.[2]

First, they react favourably to increased amounts of fertiliser. Higher quantities of nitrogenous fertiliser raise the grain yield and not the growth of leaves and stalks. HYV can absorb dosages of 100 to 120 pounds per acre. With traditional varieties on the other hand the tolerable limit is only 40 pounds per acre, more fertiliser making the ears of the long-stalked plants too heavy so that they snap and fall. HYV also use the fertiliser more intensively because they produce at least 50 per cent more cereal for each pound of fertiliser than the traditional varieties. Without the use of fertiliser the yield is the same as or lower than that of the normal varieties.

Secondly, the new varieties are less dependent on the length of day than the traditional ones. Where water is available they can be planted at any time of year in the tropic and sub-tropical regions of the world. The new types of rice ripen quicker. It has been possible to lower the ripening time from 150-180 days to 115-130 days, even to 90-100 days in some cases. This makes it possible to have three or four harvests each year.

Thirdly, the new varieties need larger quantities of fertilisers and pesticides than the traditional or local improved varieties of seed. The control of irrigation is a vital prerequisite for increasing the yield of high-yielding rice. In order to achieve four harvests in a year, sowing has to follow harvest as soon as possible. The Green Revolution is a technological and capital-intensive production system which has many socio-economic side effects.

One of the greatest evils of agriculture in developing countries is the extremely low yield per hectare. HYV have the potential to break this pattern, since under laboratory conditions they increase output three or four fold over traditional varieties. In field experiments they can double the yield. If one assumes that it is possible to produce more than one harvest each year, then the Green Revolution should be producing fantastic growth rates in grain output. Yet the desire to get rid of hunger within a few years has not been fulfilled.

In 1972, sixteen million hectares (20 per cent of the entire rice area) of South and South-East Asia was sown with new varieties of seed. In South America 0.6 million hectares out of a total of 6.5 million were sown with new rice seeds. In general, however, the introduction of new wheat varieties has caught on quicker than rice. The UN/FAO planting goals have already been reached in the wheat areas of the Far East, whereas the goals for rice, the staple crop, have not been achieved. The significant reasons for this, aside from social factors, are the inadequate water facilities and the lack of flood control.

It is not easy to answer the question to what extent the Green Revolution is the cause of the increase in harvests, since it is hardly possible to isolate the influence of HYV from other factors, such as improved weather conditions, increase in cultivated areas, improved production methods

Table 22: HYV yields for selected countries[3]

Country	Yield (kilo, hectare, approximated value)		Percentage of HYV
	1961-64	1971	Percentage of HYV
Pakistan	1400	2400	43
India	1520	1710	25
Philippines	1240	1720	56
South Vietnam	1860	2280	32

and price control. However, a fairly clear indication of both the success up to now and the future potential is shown by the rise in yields per hectare in four countries where the new varieties represent at least 25 per cent of total production.

This is a significant increase in average yields per hectare. But at the same time it can be seen that production lags far behind potential capacity. The spectacular successes under laboratory conditions are countered in practice by growing problems and setbacks. Most areas which are suitable for the HYV have now been cultivated. Any further cultivation depends on expansion of irrigation systems. It also depends on the solution of an important socio-economic problem, in that it was large farms and richer farmers who were the first to profit from HYV, and for financial and organisational reasons, small farmers often have no access to these varieties. Also, the shortage of fertilisers and fuels due to the oil crisis has made modern agriculture even more dependent on external factors.

Because of difficulties such as these, the target of raising food production in the developing nations between 1961 and 1975 by 3.4 per cent was not met in spite of the Green Revolution. The growth rates between 1961 and 1975 only rose by 2.9 per cent.

Whom does the Green Revolution benefit? Poor people in the cities have until now hardly profited at all; the prices for corn have risen despite the Green Revolution. Barbara Böttger reported a grotesque situation when in 1971/72 the stocks of the Food Corporation of India were overflowing and millions of tons of wheat were sent to Bangladesh, while at the same time Indians had as little to eat as ever and were denied the benefits of the wheat stocks.[4]

Nor was the Green Revolution any real revolution for 550 million rural people who, according to World Bank estimates, were living in absolute poverty in the Third World. Two thirds of these people came from India, Indonesia, Bangladesh and Pakistan alone. On the contrary, the new agricultural technology worked against these people. This is well illustrated by the example of East Tanjur district, Tamil Nadu, which is one of the main affected regions in South India:

By planting the HYV seeds, a middle farmer (farming twenty-five to thirty hectares) had increased his production in 1971 by 36 per cent over the figures for 1964-5, whereas a small farmer (farming less than two hectares) had an increase of 25 per cent. The difference between the two is due entirely to the greater amount of chemical fertilisers that the middle farmer could afford to put in.

In 1971, the cost of inputs such as chemical fertilisers, HYV seeds, pesticides, wages for agricultural labour was, on average, rupees 1125 per hectare. A middle farmer could borrow up to rupees 750 per hectare from the banks and co-operative societies at 8.25 per cent interest per annum. But to a small farmer the banks and co-ops never lend more than a maximum of rupees 750, irrespective of whether he cultivated more than one hectare. As a result, the small farmer could invest, on average, only rupees 350 per hectare, making up the deficiency in chemical fertilisers by using farmyard manure, which naturally led to smaller yields than those of the middle farmer. For a small farmer to borrow from private money-lenders meant having to pay 50 per cent interest per annum, this figure shooting up to 100 to 200 per cent for tenants and sharecroppers to whom the banks and co-ops never lend because they own no land which can be held as security.

By 1971 the net real income of the big farmer rose by 25 per cent over the pre-Green-Revolution 1964-65 figure. *There was no such increase for the small farmer, tenant and sharecropper*, partly because of the servicing of the debts which could not be paid back and had to be carried over from year to year and partly because of the lack of adequate inputs.[5] So in this case it was the credit mechanisms that rapidly enlarged the gap between big farmers and landowners on the one hand and small farmers and tenant farmers on the other. Whoever wishes to profit from the Green Revolution has to be prepared to invest.

Banks are hardly likely to lend money to small farmers and even co-operatives are all too often dominated by the interests of the richer classes. And so in most cases the small farmers are forced to take out private loans at extortionate rates of interest. In the event of a bad harvest they fall hopelessly into debt, lose their land to the creditor, who is often a big landowner, and sink to the level of tenants and then further to farm-workers. The last stop for many is the slums of the big cities. It is not surprising then that many small farmers are not willing to take on the risks of the Green Revolution and prefer to farm merely for their own needs.

In regions where the Green Revolution has been successful the price of land and rents goes up. For example in the Indian Punjab the proportion of the harvest that has to be paid as rent rose from 50 to 70 per cent. This forces the tenants to cultivate the new varieties. They run the greater risk, yet the landowners profit. For tenants there is not even the chance of falling back on a subsistence level economy, because the higher rents can only be met by cultivating the new varieties of cereals. Debts and the loss of tenancy are often the result. Thousands of contracts are cancelled by the landowners who, with an eye to greater profits, want to cultivate the land themselves along commercial and technological lines. This automatically increases the hardship of the landless.

One result of the Green Revolution has been the emergence of a new type of farm run along the lines of industrial concerns. In the face of this development the small farmers and tenants have even less chance than they had before under the big patriarchal landowners. Feudal landowners and the new commercial farmers have united as a new class with strong political influence which can successfully defend itself against the demands of the small farmers, tenants and farm-workers. Moreover in many cases the situation is made worse by government programmes, which strive exclusively for a maximum possible rise in production without any regard for the social consequences. As a result support is concentrated on the relatively small number of farmers with large tracts of land.

Many developing nations have easy access to credit for agricultural machinery, despite their large-scale unemployment. According to an agricultural survey in Kerala, one tractor makes forty men redundant. In Pakistan one tractor makes twelve ox ploughs redundant. In the Indian Punjab the introduction of sixty-five combine harvesters put about 20,000 harvest workers out of their jobs. In the Punjab and Bahawalpur (in Pakistan) an inquiry into sixty mechanised farming concerns revealed that the number of permanently employed workers had fallen from 2,000 to 340. Of the remaining 340, 100 were employed as tractor drivers.[6]

Mechanisation reduces the number of available work places and benefits only a few large landowners. It speeds up the development of the rural proletariat in Third World countries which have a characteristic overflow of labour. In the end it means 'development of underdevelopment'. The example of Mexico, which has a small percentage of employment in highly industrialised concerns, is a good one:

> In 1960, 54 percent of total agricultural output was produced on only 3 percent of Mexican farms. More important, in terms of the trend towards a growing polarization in the agricultural sector, this same 3 percent accounted for 80 percent of the increase in agricultural production between 1950 and 1960. It was these large-scale, capital-intensive, irrigated farms that were by far the largest beneficiaries of the new wheats.
>
> This radical increase in output and productivity in only a small part of the total agricultural economy, coupled with a rapid growth in population, meant that the number of landless labourers in rural Mexico grew from 2.3 million in 1950 to 3.3 million in 1960. Because of increased use of mechanization, the number of days worked by each labourer on average fell from 194 in 1950 to 100 in 1960, and his real income from such employment fell from $68 to $56. Even the overall growth of the economy, about 6 percent a year, has been unable to provide enough employment opportunities in the urban areas to prevent this deterioration in the rural situation.[7]

Rudolph A. Peterson amongst others comes to this conclusion as a result of his detailed analysis of fifteen developing countries in the Development Programme of the United Nations: 'The dramatic effect of the spreading knowledge that the new agriculture offers a profitable investment, sets in motion deep currents of change in the relations between agriculture, commerce and industry, and between town and country.'[8]

This movement enlarges the existing gap and is beneficial above all to the rich. Conflicts cannot fail to result from the growing social inequalities. Does this mean that the Green Revolution is turning red? The incident in Kilvenmani in Tamil Nach in 1968 when forty-two women and children rebelling against their landlords were burnt alive in their houses has become part of history.[9] There are many similar examples. 'The government and the newspapers described it as "agricultural tension" — a euphemism for class struggle, which has been intensified by the Green Revolution', wrote Mohan Ram, an Indian journalist.[10] In one of his reports, called 'The causes and nature of rural tension', he cited the Indian Minister of the Interior's conviction that, instead of being an instrument of social change, the Green Revolution had become a weapon of social repression and for that reason also a cause of new social tension.

The Green Revolution is built on a backward social structure in agriculture. Since it is primarily judged on the merit of production increases and not on social imperatives, a situation has arisen whereby the elements of disparity — instability and disorder — have increased the potential for social tension. This analysis stems from 1969. Since then it has proved to be more than correct.

It would be false to assume that the social and economic problems associated with the Green Revolution are purely confined to the developing countries. Many of the requirements of the new technology, such as capital, know-how, fertilisers, pesticides and machinery, have to be imported and so the developing countries become even more dependent on the industrialised countries. The introduction of expensive and unfitting agricultural technology increases the flow of money for debts and interest from the poor countries into the pockets of the rich. This dependence,

132

since the oil crisis, has become even more pronounced.

Erich Jacoby, Professor of Social Anthropology at the University of Stockholm, has pointed out the little understood fact that through the displacement of the greater part of the Third World agricultural employment potential into western industries producing fertilisers, other chemicals, tractors and mechanical equipment, the control of agriculture in the Third World has slipped even further. 'In other words: the work of the industrial countries produces just the equipment which contributes to the prevention of growth in agricultural employment in the Third World.'[11] The multinational agro-businesses aggravate this development failure. They control the whole chain of agricultural production from what goes in to what comes out onto the market.

Despite all that is said to the contrary, the answer does not lie in the new seeds alone. The new varieties could in theory prove to be the best option for poor farmers in areas with an excess of rural labour, since they offer greater employment possibilities and higher yields per hectare, and their genetic strains can be improved in accordance with the farmer's needs. However, to achieve this, radical social change and expensive technologies are essential. Without these the advantages of the Green Revolution will never reach the poor rural masses.

It is hopeless to wait for the redirection of privileges and other such measures to come from above, since every reform will fail as long as a new distribution of status, wealth and power is not experienced at the grass roots. Change means breaking the numerous interlocking dependencies on local landlords, money-lenders, traders and political leaders who are so often connected by their economic interests. Forms and strategies towards the self-organisation of agricultural workers, tenants and small farmers must be found and adhered to. In this way land reform can be carried through, the tenancy system altered and the peasants can benefit from the credit facilities which are — theoretically — at their disposal.

The poor would really gain power if they were allowed to administer all their requirements themselves — such as supply of high-yielding seeds, fertilisers, pesticide, advice and credit and the technical problems which arise out of the Green Revolution. Development aid programmes and extension services in the context of the Green Revolution have to be planned in such a way that they promote the initiative and social organisation of the poor people. Above all they must not be taken over by one-sided views on technological and quantitative development.

> It is not up to the peasants to participate in the nation's development under the guidance of the technicians, the young volunteers and the elite; rather the latter should participate in the development of the peasants, who themselves should be capable of a final determination on their own development. Otherwise we cannot talk about self-development but of 'developmentist' pressures which can only be imposed and are therefore bound to fail.[12]

Now that we understand that the solution to the food problem in developing countries is not just a question of increasing productivity but also depends on solving the employment problem, we can attempt to discover the appropriate technology to do this. By appropriate we do not mean the technology with the best quantitative results, but a technology suited to the existing situation. It is crucial to find a technology which increases the number of workplaces and improves the efficiency of the work, a technology developed for small-holders with between two and ten hectares. They have the greatest potential to work intensively, to use the least capital and energy and possibly to use their agricultural products in small-scale local industries. In this way their dependence on others will become as little as possible.

Of greatest importance is the production of simple water-pumps and components for small wells essential to the small farmer. The International Rice Research Institute in the

134

Philippines considers the provision of irrigation facilities to be fundamental to increasing yields. Irrigated villages can increase their output per hectare by at least half a ton, while in unirrigated areas the yields stay the same.[13]

In the technical planning of new irrigation systems the energy factor is all too often disregarded. Recent research has shown that the energy required to move water to fields distant from large reservoirs is far too expensive. Only small, local irrigation systems are financially feasible. The development of local water resources through small reservoirs and irrigation systems must take priority.

Because the agro-business dominates the international market with its propaganda about expensive technologies, the extremely important discoveries of 'appropriate' technology are often not widely known. In an attempt to change this situation, the FAO magazine *Ceres*, in a special section on 'knowledge and technology', gives great emphasis to its reports on technological research and discoveries which would otherwise never get a hearing.

IR-8, the first rice varieties made available by the IRRI in the late nineteen sixties, heralded the Green Revolution. But these varieties were liable to damage and disease and therefore tended once again indirectly to benefit the well-off farmers who could afford pesticides. In the meantime research has produced results more favourable to the poor farmers.

The IRRI has a seed-plasma bank containing an estimated 30,000 of the world's 100,000 varieties of rice seed. The plasma comes from local varieties whose yields are very low but which have become adapted over thousands of years to the environmental conditions, such as saline soils, flood or drought. They have developed resistance to disease and damage. These traditional varieties are now being crossed systematically with new high yielding varieties. By 1973 IR-26, which was immune to the seven worst diseases and pests, had been produced.

Other new cross-breeds which have already been made available are more or less immune to a broad range of damage and disease. Trials with cross-breeds suitable for dry areas are already far advanced. Experiments have begun on varieties that will survive in salty earth. This means hope for millions of farmers who live in coastal areas which are regularly flooded by the sea. Five-metre-high 'flood rice', which can be harvested by boat in flooded regions, also seems to be a real possibility. In a few years farmers in cool regions should be able to cultivate HYV. It should even be possible to cultivate rice on slopes where water cannot be dammed. Finally it is hoped to raise the protein content of rice from 8 to 10 per cent without harming the yield. This would help make up the protein deficiency in the diet of the poorest levels of society in the developing nations.

Another important area of research is to find ways in which plants can fix nitrogen direct from the atmosphere, thereby reducing the need for fertilisers. This has been achieved with rice plants. There is a mechanism whereby nitrogen can be absorbed from the air and transported to the roots by bacteria which exist in the atmospheric state and which the plants can absorb. Absorption mechanisms are also being developed in new breeds.[14]

It is possible, or so it seems, to lay down a blueprint for action on the world food crisis. That is what we have attempted to do in chapter 8. But in practice can the ideas discussed there be applied in time?

The political arrangements that now dominate the Third World do not in sum present a vision of hope. Neither do the attitudes of the rich countries which cling selfishly to the needs of their own economic advance. Yet if there were the will on both sides dramatic changes could be accomplished. And to demonstrate the validity of this we plan to look at different parts of the world where the small-scale peasant farmers have been made or are being made the thrusting edge of development. We do not wish to suggest at this point that we agree or disagree with the methods used. We reserve our opinion on that for our concluding chapter.

Japan

The fascination of Japan is its success — the first Asian country which transformed its rural sector into a dynamo of small-scale activity. It began where most of the Asian countries have to begin — with a feudal society dominated by hierarchical relationships. Its level of productivity was probably not very different from, at best only moderately higher than, levels of productivity found today throughout Asia. Average farm size was small. Much of the Japanese success was achieved within the constraints of the old order. Much was achieved by critical changes to parts of it. *Most important, however, was the fact that the breakthrough to high production was made without transformation to large-scale agriculture.*

In 1878 the farm size was approximately one hectare and the yield of husked rice was about 1.8 metre tons per hectare.

137

By 1960 the yield was 4 metre tons per hectare yet farm size was still small, in fact as low as 8 hectares. During this time the annual growth rate of agriculture's net output averaged almost 2.3 per cent and the expansion of food crops was high enough to outstrip the growth rate of population. Even more impressively, the number of people on the land changed only slightly. Between 1878 and 1912 the total agricultural work force changed from 15.5 million to 14.5 million.

Agriculture's achievement played a critical role in the development of the rest of the Japanese economy. Japan was self-sufficient in food and could resist the pressures of inflation arising from food shortages. Tea and silk became important earners of foreign exchange, making it possible for Japan to buy in the tools of industrialisation. Finally the agricultural sector was, for a number of decades, the principal source of revenue for the central government and in turn government expenditure played an important role in the provision of services and facilities for the agricultural sector.

Before the Meiji Restoration (1868) — the event that marked the beginning of the era of rapid reform — the fiscal structure of Japan was based on rice taxes paid in kind by the peasant to the feudal lords. These amounted to 35 per cent of the crop. The Restoration changed all this. In 1871 all land was made freely cultivable. And in 1872 it was declared to be freely transferable. The feudal title of 35 per cent was abolished and in its place a new land tax was introduced — payable to the government at about the same rate as before. Now, however, it went into the government coffers and was spent on large-scale improvements both to the agrarian and to the urban economy. Unfortunately the heavy burden of the land tax, the need to pay it in cash rather than kind, compelled many a small farmer to sell his land and accept tenancy under a landowner. Too often the place of feudalism was taken over by a new landlordism.

In commercial terms however the new landlordism was a progressive one. Since landlords received their rents in rice they had a vested interest in improving its quality — then they received a better price in the market. Moreover since the government's rake-off was a constant amount it encouraged the landlords to increase production so as to increase their capital. A good proportion of these new landowners' savings found their way into the new sprouting industries. During all this time the price of rice was rising and this too was an incentive to produce more.

By and large in this first round of land reform the distribution of land between owner-cultivator and tenants was maintained. But the way was open for large-scale changes in agricultural technique — land improvement, better irrigation and drainage techniques, superior seeds, improved methods of crop cultivation, increased use of pesticides and fertilisers. All these things began to be introduced fairly rapidly.

Although there was some early fascination with American and German agricultural methods these were quickly found to be inapplicable to the Japanese small-holder situation. Increasingly they relied on indigenous research. Methods of farming were evolved which required relatively little investment of fixed capital but which made full use of the abundant labour resources.

Average yield for the six staple crops increased nearly by 70 per cent between 1880 and 1930. Net real output of the agricultural sector increased by approximately 150 per cent between 1880 and 1938. However it is estimated that inputs only increased by 30 per cent. Thus technological advance made a major contribution to the increase in agricultural productivity. But despite all these breakthroughs the course of Japanese agricultural advance did not run smooth. At the time of the First World War the rate of growth dipped. Food shortages developed and there was not enough food to feed the growing urban population.

The landownership system and the size of holdings now seemed as if they were becoming a limiting factor. It was Japan's defeat in the Second World War which provided the possibility of a new breakthrough. The American occupation administration, anxious to break up concentrations of power in Japanese society, set in motion a far-reaching agrarian reform that reduced the number of tenants and virtually eliminated absentee ownership. The economic incentives of the tenants were sharply increased. All farmland owned by absentee landlords and all farmland leased by resident landlords in excess of one hectare was bought by the government and redistributed.

The land reform programme was begun in 1947 and completed in 1949. As one would expect the landlords fought bitterly to slow it down. They challenged the law in the courts, arbitrarily evicted tenants assuming they were not strong enough to resist, subdivided large estates among family members and so on. But the presence of a determined occupying force helped to push the scheme through. About two million hectares of farmland — amounting to 80 per cent of the total cultivated land — was transferred to tenants.

The end result of these reforms was another great surge forward in Japanese agriculture. However we should note that there were certain other contributing factors: the dissolution of the Japanese Empire ended colonial competition; food shortages on the world markets; new advances in technology; and a much more active government role in land reclamation and improvement.

In assessing the great achievements of Japanese agriculture it is important not to underplay the enormous back-up service provided by the government in return for its one third levy. The organisation and systematic pursuit of agricultural research is one important example. And this was matched by a well organised extension service that took the new technology out into the villages. Unlike the majority of developing countries the extension agents usually lived in the villages they served. There were also the strong supporting institutions for the smaller farmers. Recognising that they were economically the weakest sector in the community and that they often faced great difficulties in marketing their product advantageously or in obtaining credit, the government helped to establish a highly efficient network of co-operatives. Now nearly all the farmers belong to these and they extend into the smallest hamlet bringing credit and marketing facilities to virtually every farmer.

Finally there was the education system itself. Universal literacy came early to Japan. As early as 1879 44 per cent of children of elementary school age were in school. More important still was the rapid expansion of 'technical supplementary schools'. Most of these gave great emphasis to topics useful to agriculture. Agriculture was not regarded as second best but as a key element in the development of a new Japanese society.

There is one other aspect of the Japanese development experience that is crucially relevant: the application of labour-intensive techniques in the non-agricultural sector. Many of the important new industries were actually located in the countryside — not just agriculture-related industries like processing, silk-reeling and -weaving, but industries of a more varied character. In many instances small-scale industries were lined up with the larger and more capital-intensive industries through the production of components.

Although the story of Japanese agriculture is one of a remarkable success it is important not to forget that Japan has at least three advantages over other countries trying to do the same thing today. First, although the population was growing it did so only at a rate of 0.7 to 1.5 per cent — about the same as in Europe during the early stages of economic development. These rates just do not compare with what is happening today. Secondly, Japan's first initiative was taken at a time of rapidly growing agricultural trade. Thirdly, Japan has a well-watered and temperate climate. Even so Japan's methods have been transported successfully to the very different climate of Taiwan, though only after a fairly lengthy period of research.

Set against these advantages is the fact that modern technology is now much more advanced than when Japan began her agricultural revolution. Yields can be raised much faster today than was conceivable in Japan a century ago. Perhaps what is lost on the roundabouts can be won on the swings.

Tanzania

Tanzania is remarkable not for what it has done but for what
it is doing and what it intends to do. It appears to be the one
developing country today apart from China that has
unambiguously decided that its principal hope for development lies in its villages. One of the poorest countries in
Africa — it has a per capita income of only eighty-six dollars
— it has under the leadership of its first president, Julius
Nyerere, consciously set out to evolve a policy of
development that emphasises the poor man at the expense of
the town-dweller. Salaries of politicians and civil servants
have been cut, university students have been enrolled *en
masse* into a national service corps that is sent into the
villages for a year's service, school curriculae have been
rewritten so that agriculture becomes a principal subject
and the President himself constantly emphasises the goals of
rural development and whenever possible leaves his desk
to go out and dig irrigation ditches — or whatever task is at
hand.

This agricultural development policy evolves around what
are called *ujamaa* villages. (Literally translated, this means
'familyhood'.) Nyerere has argued that the traditional
scattered small-holdings of much of the Tanzanian countryside are an unsuitable form of rural settlement. They make
the communication of ideas difficult and people become too
individualistic. But if they come together in villages, he
argues, and pool their land they can more easily maximise
their productivity. Farmers can be reached with credit,
advice and expertise. A dispensary can be built. So can a
school. Machinery such as mills and tractors can be shared
and the overhead costs of running them distributed more
easily. The farmers can be organised into co-operatives
which will arrange both the purchase of new seeds and
fertilisers and the sales and marketing of their output.

There was one other important element in the *ujamaa*
villages: that they should be infused with the spirit of the
Arusha Declaration. This declaration, written principally
by Nyerere, was adopted by Tanzania's single political

142

party, TANU, at a party congress in 1967. Its philosophy is summed up by something Nyerere wrote as early as 1962:

> Acquisitiveness for the purpose of gaining power and prestige is unsocialist. In an acquisitive society wealth tends to corrupt those who possess it. It tends to breed in them a desire to live more comfortably than their fellows, to dress better and in every way to outdo them. They begin to feel they must climb as far above their neighbours as they can. The visible contrast between their own comfort and the comparative discomfort of the rest of society becomes almost essential to the enjoyment of their wealth, and this sets off the spiral of personal competition — which is then anti-social.
>
> Both the 'rich' and the 'poor' individual were completely secure in African society. Natural catastrophe brought famine, but it brought famine to everybody — 'poor' or 'rich'. Nobody starved, either of food or of human dignity, because he lacked personal wealth; he could depend on the wealth possessed by the community of which he was a member. That was socialism. That is socialism. There can be no such thing as acquisitive socialism, for that would be another contradiction in terms. Socialism is essentially distributive. Its concern is to see that those who sow reap a fair share of what they sow.[1]

That is the theory. And the practice?

It is only recently that such a large percentage of Tanzania's population has entered the new villages — as recently as early 1974 only 16 per cent of the people lived in them. Nyerere has now declared that the entire rural population must be living in villages by 1976. Inevitably despite Nyerere's own sensitive and caring leadership, local officials, anxious to fill their quotas of new villages, have used dubious methods. Houses have been burnt down and old fields ploughed up to prevent people returning.

The results have not been propitious for Tanzania. Food production has plummeted. Most of this is a result of two

143

years of drought in 1973 and 1974, but some is also a consequence of the disruption in the farming system brought about by these large-scale upheavals. But rains in 1975 have given the scheme a great boost and outside observers, the World Bank, for example, see real progress.

Despite the relatively harsh environment the *ujamaa* villages have a number of compensatory attractions. The villages receive priority in the allocation of extension personnel, water development, health facilities, schools and co-operative services. And once they are fully established they are eligible for production credit. This is the principal difference between *ujamaa* and the Chinese system. One depends principally on incentive (although this is beginning to change), the other, at least for a time, on an element of compulsion. Yet for all the political pushing that has gone on the *ujamaa* villages are still very much in an early stage. There is collective farming but it probably rèprèsents less than 1 per cent of the total cultivated area. And where there are *ujamaa* shambas yields are constantly reported to be less than the yields on private plots. There are many indications too which suggest that people are 'going *ujamaa*' not so much because they believe in the communal ideal but because of the priority accorded the villages in government services.

Goran Hyden, Professor in the Department of Political Science at the University of Dar es Salaam, believes that many of the basic principles of *ujamaa* are not being adhered to in practice.[2] Instead of an 'Arusha' attitude of self-reliance there is a great danger that villagers are becoming more, not less, dependent on government. Government officials are often sent to organise the construction of local amenities — a task which could usually be organised just as effectively by peasants when they are not needed for work on the fields.

Also it is the regional officials who set the investment targets for each village and not the peasants themselves. In many cases these bureaucratic officers are out of touch with the resource needs and the potential productivity of an area. Mismanagement occurs and farmers feel frustrated that the decision-making is taken out of their hands.

Since the beginning of 1974 the government has placed great emphasis on the need to move people into *ujamaa* villages at any cost. Moving is no longer a matter of providing incentives — it has become compulsory. According to Hyden, if resistance is met, then those farmers' homesteads are often burnt down. In early 1975 the government gave up its insistence on communal production and byelaws have been introduced which make food-cropping compulsory. In the 1970s the Tanzanian agricultural policy favoured cash crops and the result has been low prices and a drop in production of food crops. To restore the food output the government has been forced into a more practical and less ideological strategy of development. Tanzania is dropping its insistence on socialist goals and voluntary participation to achieve those goals. Instead a measure of coercion is creeping into the system.

Yet for all the deficiencies and mistakes the *ujamaa* villages do offer the possibility of real agricultural change. The basic conception is good. The political leadership of the country is fully committed to their success. And new ideas are welcome. It is by no means an open and shut situation.

Certainly it is an enormous improvement on the old colonial pattern of agricultural development inherited by Tanzania when it became independent in 1962. The British introduced high priced export crops like tobacco, coffee and tea. This did increase the level of incomes quite sharply. But is also built up concentrations of wealth in small pockets of the country. Moreover peasant farmers who grew cash crops often neglected their production of food crops, preferring to buy these in the market place. The cash economy began to take over and one of the ironies of this kind of development is that it is the areas with the most successful cash cropping that have the highest outmigration to the town. Peasants who have money, it seems, are more attracted to the bright lights than those who don't.

The *ujamaa* concept is more sensibly based. By trying to emphasise village culture and social potential it will do something to bring the facilities of the bright lights to the country-side. Also, as Nyerere sees it, these villages will be less dependent on the outside cash economy. They will grow their own food crops and introduce new sources of food like fruit trees, chickens and cows. Small scale industries will be introduced — carpentry, grain and oil milling, charcoal and brick manufacture, textile and ginning. In this way it will be possible to develop the economy in situ without the enormous social upheavals that result when there is long distance migration and large scale industrialisation and division of labour.

Tanzania also sees the need for regional growth centres — small towns that can both absorb the surplus rural population — for obviously in the long run there is a limit to the numbers the country-side can hold — and provide counter magnets to the pull of the metropolis.

The World Bank, attempting to put into practice its new commitment to the small farmer has been investigating the potential of these *ujamaa* villages and its observation on their potential are encouraging for Tanzania.

The Bank is planning to back financially an *ujamaa* village scheme involving 250,000 people in the Kigoma region. The Bank's financial contribution will be spent on the inputs of new improved seed and fertilizer, marketing and credit systems, extension services, agricultural research, social services, irrigation and access roads. This aid will amount to $225 per family of which Tanzania will provide 25%.

World Bank officials are confident that within 10 years village and family income can be doubled. (At the moment per capita annual income in Kigoma is $20, well below Tanzania's average). Moreover they reckon that the economic rate of return on the project will be 22% a year — which, of course, is well above what a private investor would hope to get out of the average industrial enterprise. (Admittedly however his risks in industry would be much lower).

Although these figures suggest that the World Bank officials have an enormous amount of confidence in the potential of peasant farming, *ujamaa* style, it should be noted that calculations of this kind are highly sensitive. If yields increased by 75% instead of the planned 100% the rate of return would be zero! And if they increased by 80% the rate of return would be only 5%.

146

It is really too early to say whether the *ujamaa* villages will succeed or not. After all the *ujamaa* villages are but seven years old as a concept and most of them are younger than that. But the omens are good. It is hopefully only a question of time.

Even if *ujamaa* itself fails an important step forward will have been taken. Agriculture is clearly the priority of Tanzania — that itself is an important step forward. Even if Tanzania has to end up relying on individual peasants farming and responding to material incentives it is relatively simple to prohibit richer peasants from emerging and buying out the others. All that is needed is a law prohibiting the hiring of labour. If a peasant is firmly limited in that way then he will be able to develop his initiative and enterprise only to the point where it does not intrude on the wider ambitions and purpose of society. *Ujamaa* certainly should be tried, but if it fails there is a good second-best alternative to fall back on.

Brazil

Brazil is one of the few countries in the developing world that still have a plentiful supply of land on which continued expansion of output can be achieved, even without significant improvements in agricultural technology. And after a long period during which the government has given all its emphasis to industrialisation, it is now shifting gear to throw much more of its resources in the direction of agriculture. The government believes that with industrial capacity almost fully utilised it will be easier to sustain high rates of overall economic growth if agricultural growth rates of 6 or 7 per cent are achieved. The government also believes that, given the relative abundance of land and labour, it can expand agriculture with a lower investment rate than would be possible with a heavier reliance on industry.

The government feel that for the foreseeable future the best chances for increasing productivity and output lie in aiding the larger farmers in the better-off regions. Thus most of the governmental support is going to go to the already successful commercial farmers.

This approach may well solve Brazil's food problem in the round. But it will do nothing for the regional disparities. It will do nothing to stop urban drift — it could exacerbate it. It will certainly do nothing for the poor. With Sao Paulo and Rio de Janeiro skyscrapering into the air it is sometimes difficult to remember just how abysmally poor much of Brazil still is. Yet 23 million Brazilians suffer from hookworm; 185 million have goitre; 1 million trachoma; 600,000 leprosy. A child dies every forty-two seconds and every ten years 6 million Brazilians under sixteen years of age are taken to the cemetery.

The north-east, although not Brazil's poorest region, is the one with the most severe and intractable social problems. It is said that its land distribution is the most unequal in the world. In the state of Marauhao 71 per cent of farmers have only 3.9 per cent of the wealth, whereas 1.2 per cent have 61.5 per cent. In Pernambuco 65.3 per cent of the small farmers have 4.6 per cent of the wealth, leaving 61.7 per cent for only 2.4 per cent. In Rio Grande do Norte 58.4 per cent have 3.8 per cent of the wealth and 1.8 per cent have 60.3 per cent.

The system of *latifundia* (large estates) and share-cropping still operates much the same as it did four hundred years ago.

In one of the north-eastern states — Rio Grande do Norte — the World Bank is establishing a new pilot project to see if it is possible, despite all the impediments, historical and present, to make small-holder peasant farming work. The fact that the World Bank has been allowed to do this is no doubt because of the amount of favour they have won in aiding over the years Brazil's more conventional growth policies. Yet, despite this caveat, it is worth looking at what they are trying to do if only to see the nature of the problems that such an attempt raises.

The Bank project is set in the drought polygon of Brazil. Apart from a narrow coastal strip the rainfall is poor and erratic. At least once a decade there is an extreme drought and thousands upon thousands of destitute people pour into the towns seeking work and relief. Population is growing at

148

2.9 per cent a year, reduced to 1.5 per cent through emigration. The per capita income is about 180 dollars a year compared with Brazil's average 600 dollars. And for the poorest half of the population it is nearer 50 dollars.

Many of the large *haciendas* are underutilised. Owners are often absent. Share-croppers have to surrender one third to half their cash crop (usually cotton) in lieu of rent. Crop yields are going down because of the ravages of erosion and the decline in soil fertility. The regional government is badly organised, operating on a hand-to-mouth basis. Policies and personnel change frequently. Extension agents in the countryside sometimes fail to get paid for three to six months at a time. Agricultural research is limited. There is one small one-man cotton research station and a two-man coconut research station. Even here fertilisers have only been in use since 1973.

Until 1974 the government's principal strategy has been to try to create jobs in the industrial sector. Using fiscal incentives it has only, since 1960, been able to create fifteen thousand jobs a year. And each job cost it 12,000 dollars. This is a very expensive way to develop a depressed region and one of the aims of the World Bank is to show just how much cheaper it will be to create jobs in the rural sector.

The Bank's project will attempt to work with 35,000 farmers. It will have four main aims. First, establishment of four marketing crops; second, a significant expansion in extension services; third, a simplification of credit procedures and the availability of this credit together with technological inputs (fertiliser; insecticide, improved seeds, etc.) plus supporting services for small producers and share-croppers; fourth, health training, nutrition.

Although the aim of the project is to reach the share-croppers and *minifundistas* (small holdings), it has at least two weaknesses. First, in its initial steps at least, it has accepted that it can do little for the landless and for those with plots of land too small to be economic. And secondly it has accepted that for the next few years it will not be able to alter the archaic and debilitating system of land tenure, that politically it would be counter-productive to push for such fundamental changes. Perhaps, it is argued, these limitations can be overcome by a number of innovative measures: first by providing certain counterbalancing institutions such as co-operatives for the share-croppers; secondly, by introducing some form of contractual arrangement enforceable in the courts between landlord and tenant that will give the tenant a fair return for any improvements he might make. Possibly once a certain impetus to agricultural improvement has been introduced it will be easier to implement the far-reaching land reform statutes already on the law books.

This, if you like, is rural development the hard way. Yet it is with this kind of project — and the Tanzania one — that the World Bank wants to assist the governments of the developing countries in a world-wide drive to get the output of peasant small-holders increasing by 5 per cent a year by 1985. It remains to be seen if it can be done in a country where the political institutions are so heavily weighted against the poor.

Eire

In a word Ireland's problem is that of emigration. Ireland has seen her population fall in a hundred years from eight to four million. The impetus behind the initial large-scale migrations was the Great Famine of 1845-49. A million people emigrated in half a dozen years.

Emigration began as an economic need in a moment of distress. But it evolved to a point at which the principal cause of emigration was prior emigration. As the young people paid less attention to work on the land, so the old people found the work increasingly difficult, became less able to take agricultural initiatives and less receptive to new agricultural ideas. So there seemed more reason for the next generation of young to depart. The most important spur of all was the picture painted by those already gone. The letters from America in the nineteenth century, albeit written from overcrowded tenements in New York and Chicago, spoke of a glorious land. Maurice O'Sullivan wrote in *Twenty Years*

150

A-Growing, that delicate and beautiful classic of Gaelic
literature, of how, when he was growing up in an Irish
village, 'I looked west at the edge of the sky where America
should be lying, and I slipped back on the paths of thought.
It seemed to me now that the New Island was before me with
its fine streets and great high houses, some of them so tall that
they scratched the sky; gold and silver out in the ditches and
nothing to do but gather it . . . I see the boys and girls who
were once my companions . . . .'

Once emigration reaches endemic proportions, as it has in
Ireland a kind of depression, a despair, sets in. It was George
Bernard Shaw, Irish himself of course, who wrote that Ireland
is 'a place of futility, failure and endless pointless talk'.
Many in Ireland who know its country ways best would not
dispute that; they would merely say it was the inheritance
of so much emigration. So many have left, often the
brightest and best, who became presidents and poets in other
lands, that the population at home has been unbalanced. In a
recent survey of 231 households in the west of Ireland, it was
found that 52 people were living by themselves: 13 widows
3 widowers, 4 spinsters and 32 bachelors. Perhaps the saddest
group of all were the bachelors: most were older men who
had not the economic wherewithal, or perhaps the courage,
to ask a girl to marry them. James Healy wrote in *The Death
of an Irish Town*: 'Today whole villages around Charlestown
— for centuries the spawning streams of the people of Mayo
and Sligo — are silted by depopulation and where in my
memory there were shoals of children, more populous than
the salmon parr in the town's rich river, no child plays and
there is no promise of a child.'

There are however some fragmentary signs of hope. One
of these can be found in Glencolumbkille, a village stuck out
on the westernmost tip of Donegal. The people here tell you
their next parish is New York. So indeed it might be. It is
archetypal emigration country where the bones of the earth
stick through the starved skin. Yet now it is one of the very
few areas in the west of Ireland that is actually holding its
population. It is the home of one of the world's most
imaginative rural development schemes and its architect

is Father James McDyer, the rough-hewn, country-born parish priest. 'The key to progress in the West', McDyer says, 'is to break down the myth of emigration — that a better life can be had somewhere else.' Much of the incentive to emigrate, he argues, is not economic, but social. 'Young people have been led to believe they need urban type entertainment, the bright lights. So I say let's give it to them.' His first task eighteen years ago was to build a community hall for social activities. And it was all built by voluntary labour. 'From the day we cut the first sod,' Father McDyer recounts, 'until we formally opened it, the time lapse was precisely twelve weeks . . . I maintain that in a voluntary operation, the chief instigator should take an active part even engage in the most menial tasks. This I did, and found that morale was kept at a high level throughout.'

Now the community hall is an established part of community life. Drama — McDyer himself produces three plays each winter — films, badminton, card games, lectures and of course ceilidhs — evenings that start at 11 p.m. and finish at 3 a.m. where Irish music and dancing still hold both young and old alike. McDyer's next achievement was a successful fight for electricity and piped water to be brought into his valley.

But the backbone of the economic life of the community is a number of co-operative enterprises. There is a knitting co-op. of eighty women making Donegal sweaters, a hand-weaving tweed factory employing fifteen weavers, a machine-knitting factory, a silverwork factory and a shop in Dublin near fashionable Grafton Street to sell some of the output. The fishing industry, abandoned in the early part of the century, is being revitalised. A salmon-canning factory is in full production and recently McDyer called the first meeting of local people interested in starting a boat-building industry. Vegetable-growing, which hardly existed in former times, is now a major enterprise. That too supports a canning factory. Tough mountain pasture has been fertilised and is now holding a greater density of sheep. In the last few years, McDyer has put a large part of his energies into the tourist industry. The danger of course with tourism is that absentee entrepreneurs move in and the spin-off into the local economy is much reduced. But in Glencolumbkille the local people have built twenty thatched cottages and are renting them at up to £35 a week in the high season. And despite the general drop in tourism in Ireland because of the political situation they have maintained a 60 per cent occupancy rate throughout the year. Soon after these cottages were established, the combined co-operatives bought a local hotel that came on the market. There is now no manager and the staff run it themselves.

McDyer's thoughts are now focused on the organisation of a communal farming enterprise. There are four thousand farms in south-west Donegal that have an average farm income of a mere £138 a year. McDyer has persuaded 112 of these unproductive farmers to sink their lot in a communal farm. This would provide 18,000 acres of undivided mountain and 1,200 acres of lowland. The farm would be run by the younger men and it would give, McDyer argues, 'perpetual security and ownership for the present holders and their heirs, maximum full-time employment and the greatest possible productivity'. The Agricultural Institute and the Irish Agricultural Organisation Society have passed it as economically viable.

Despite McDyer's undoubted success, there is a certain cynicism about his methods among politicians and economists in Dublin. One influential economist has argued that if every village in the west of Ireland produced at the rate of the valley of Glencolumbkille, the agricultural market would become quickly depressed. This of course is true. But for all practical purposes, the argument is long-range and irrelevant. The more pressing need is to keep Ireland's population intact so as to provide a viable base for national economic activity. And there is enough room in the agricultural market for quite a number of Glencolumbkilles before prices are affected.

It is sad to think that if McDyer's methods had been tried a century or even forty years ago, emigration might have been seriously curtailed before it did the damage it did. In those days it would have been easier to make rural development work. Worldly consumer values were not so developed and

153

village or valley self-sufficiency would have been much easier to attain. What is significant is that after a hundred years of continuous haemorrhage, McDyer's methods can actually make an impact.

Bangladesh

Bangladesh, at the beginning of August 1974 during the latest flood disaster. The international press is full of reports on the growing corruption and imminent economic bankruptcy of the country. Is there any point in trying to unearth models for development in such a hopeless situation? René Dumont has anticipated the answer to that question:

> Technically speaking the agricultural potentialities of Bangladesh, by square mile of arable land, are much higher of those of India, China and Japan. The quality of soil and the average amount of rainfall are much higher than in India. The climate does not know any real winter, like the majority of China and Japan. Floods are the biggest constraint, but if all the potential for flood-free areas in summer, and irrigation in winter (with much higher reserves, by desilting rivers and tanks) would be used, the agricultural production of Bangladesh could be at *least doubled*, even assuming present cropping patterns, continuing dominance of rice and the use of established techniques.
> By multiple cropping, *diversification* of crops, full development of fisheries, productive trees on hills, vegetable gardening, fodder and animal production intensification, etc. . . . the actual production could be at least trebled. Technically speaking, it is *not true* to say that the future of Bangladesh is without any hope.[3]

The greatest obstacles to development are the present socio-economic structures. The income of more than 85 per cent of the population is dependent on agriculture, which produces only 58 per cent of the gross national product. About 20 per cent of the people (13.5 million) own only

154

an acre or less of land. They struggle for shared leases or work as farm-workers for many months in the year. The small farmers with one to seven acres of land make up 70 per cent of the population, 47 million people. Many try to improve their incomes by renting more land. A big proportion of this section of society is hopelessly in debt because they are exploited by private suppliers of credit and, when selling their products, by middlemen. Only 10 per cent of the population (6.8 million) belongs to the rich class owning more than seven acres of land which dominates all arrangements for tenancies and credit, all trade and manufacturing industries. The problem of how to improve the incomes and production capacity of the small farmers, tenants and farm-workers has become the central question for the survival of the young nation. The government is trying to draw up plans to help these people but the lack of finance is a tremendous drawback for the realisation of their ambitious schemes. Another hindrance to development is the rigid vertical structures of Bangladesh society, to which the lower levels of society are also bound. In addition the rich upper class has elbowed its way in between the government programmes and the grass roots level. The rich know exactly how to wield the lever of political power in order to defend their privileges and to block the interests of the weak.

Until recently the Comilla Project was one of the most quoted and studied development models. We have tried to find out how this project has stood the test of the crisis years in the young state of Bangladesh and what job it can do within the framework of new plans for development.

The story of the Comilla Rural Development Academy was stamped with the personality of Akhter Hameed Khan who was named first director of the Academy in 1958. He was in charge of the Academy until 1971. (Under pressure of political events he had to leave Bangladesh during the war for independence because he was a West Pakistani by birth.)[4]

From the beginning the Academy was conceived as an institution for both training and research, in order to unite theory and practice as closely as possible. Comilla Thana[5] with an area of 100 square miles and 150,000 inhabitants was put at its disposal as a social and agricultural laboratory. The Academy team began its work with a thorough stock-taking of the most important economic and social factors, such as land ownership, means of credit, agricultural production, marketing, industry, schools, illiteracy, the status of women etc. The results formed the basis for working out a new model of administration and extensive development projects. British colonialism had left behind the police station as the symbol of its administration. Comilla created as the new symbol the Thana Training and Development Centre (TTDC).

Co-ordination was made easier by putting the administration of government departments such as agriculture, cattle-breeding, fish-breeding, health and education under one roof in one building. At the same time this building played the part of a training centre for civil servants, political leaders and farmers and allowed all these people to participate in a common learning process through the development programme.

Inquiries established that the most urgent requirement for agricultural development was the construction of drainage systems and roads to provide access to the markets. The Academy helped with the establishment of a Rural Work Programme. The realisation of the plans was made possible because the materials were provided by the American Aid Programme PL 480 (see chapter 5). This programme was able temporarily to solve the paradoxical situation where thousands were sitting around unoccupied while the most urgent work to improve basic existence remained undone. The programme did bring temporary employment and earnings but in the long term however it made no contribution to a solution of the unemployment problem, even working to the benefit of the landowners. Better drainage and road connections raised the value of the land thereby making rents higher for tenants.

The next step was the introduction of irrigation. The Academy took over the planning of this complex undertaking. This entailed the training of working groups in the villages, the installation of tube-wells and pumps, maintenance of machinery, training drivers and mechanics etc.

After a test phase the model had developed so well that it could also be adopted in other Thanas. With a limited amount of capital and using low-cost techniques it soon became possible to irrigate several hundred thousand acres of land. In this way cereals could be cultivated in the dry season and this markedly improved living standards in those areas continuously hit by monsoon floods. At the same time new jobs were created. For a number of years this programme really captured the enthusiasm of the people.

Comilla combined an improvement of the technical infrastructure with an attempt to create new social structures which would promote development. The appropriate method seemed to be the establishment of co-operatives. These were to be used above all as a means for education, to acquaint farmers with new methods of agriculture. In parallel with this the co-operatives provided farmers with vital inputs: credits, fertilisers, pesticides, seeds and the technology that goes with these inputs. In addition the cooperatives also offered an alternative marketing system for the small farmers and tenants to replace exploitation by the creditors, landowners and middlemen. They were not therefore meant to be merely a means to produce more but also offered small farmers a means of protection and solidarity. No longer were they to be helpless individuals cheated and exploited by the powerful.

The cooperatives had to show small farmers how to build up capital. 'We were teaching them the basic principles of capitalism', wrote Akhter Hameed Khan, namely to save and to invest. It would have been hopeless to question the system as a whole. In this way the small farmers were at least able to profit from it. The village cooperatives received support through the Thana Cooperative Association which apart from providing the necessary inputs also more importantly functioned as a forum for discussion and as a training centre. It was here that representatives of the village cooperatives were able to exchange experiences and to be trained in new methods.

A new training method was developed. Each village co-operative chose from among its members a 'Model Farmer' who each week attended a course at the Thana Training Centre. Back home in his own fields the farmer would try to apply what he had learned at the training centre and try to pass on his knowledge to his fellow villagers.

Alongside these *agricultural* cooperatives other ones were built up for craftsmen, rickshaw coolies, drivers etc. In 1970 an attempt was begun to combine credit and marketing in order to eliminate the middlemen in dairy-farming, poultry-breeding etc. The Comilla Project did not only try to raise production but also to take all basic essentials for the life of the population into consideration and to improve them. Health, nutrition, accommodation, family planning and education, are all integrated in the project. What had been tried out in the 'laboratory' of the Comilla Thana, was extended to all areas of the Comilla District in several phases between 1965 and 1968.

Finally, under the title, Rural Integrated Development Programme, the Comilla Project was declared a national development programme in May 1971. After the War of Independence the plan also received the support of the new government. The Comilla experiment and its principles should lay the groundwork for the future agricultural development of Bangladesh. An official document summarises the aims of the plan as follows:

The Integrated Rural Development Program (IRDP) is committed to replication of Comilla Model Cooperatives throughout the country. It is not merely a 'Cooperative Programme'. It proceeds from a political and social philosophy and a strong set of operating principles . . . It emanates from a deep commitment to a rural society controlled by small farmers. The . . . cooperatives had been envisaged as a vehicle for economic development enabling the farmers to rally together for protecting

themselves from domination by landlords and money-
lenders, develop new leadership to challenge the
traditional vested interests and to create an institutional
infrastructure for sustaining the pace of development.
To achieve these objectives the inherent preconditions
to be fulfilled are discipline, professional management,
continuous training and an assured degree of Governmental
assistance and support.[6]

Without doubt the Comilla Project has managed
successfully to combine important factors for development.
A staff of experts and the necessary financial means are
available for the Academy. But will the experiment stand
up to the rougher conditions outside the 'laboratory'?
Director Akhter Hameed Khan himself said that there have
been enormous growing pains. The Director saw their main
cause as over-hasty expansion. But according to the plans
of the new government the Integrated Rural Development
Programme now has to be introduced into fifty Thanas each
year! In June 1973 there were 9,915 village cooperatives with
247,000 members. In May 1974, 14,000 of these cooperatives
with 373,645 members had been registered. It may be possible
in the short term to increase production in this way. But the
programme runs the danger of putting the quantity of
development before the quality of development. The
cooperatives may increasingly become service centres for
credit, seeds, fertilisers etc. which the better placed farmers
will know how to use. But the essence of the programme,
which is to give control to the small farmers, will not be
realised.
    One serious criticism of the Comilla Project is that in the
long term it has often worked to the advantage of the richer
farmers. Credits are concentrated in the hands of the most
influential members. Farmers with the largest proportion
of land draw the largest sums of money and statistics show
that they are the slowest to pay back their loans. In this
way, often intentionally, they hinder the functions of the
cooperative. It has been proved that the cooperatives with
the best rates of repayment have been the smallest

cooperatives in terms of land-ownership, private capital and membership. However, where the richer farmers have taken control of the administration, there are few opportunities left for the small farmers. They remain dependent on private money-lenders and inevitable debt hampers any initiative. These failings do not put the principles of the Comilla Project into question. But new methods have to be found which will bring political and social power to all those levels of the population which are now shut out of the decision-making process. Only in this way can they be integrated into the development programme. The responsible government departments are studying the problem. For example there are plans to bar the richer farmers from full membership of the cooperatives and to guarantee the small farmers and tenants the majority holding.

Improvements to the existing institutions are possible, although organisational measures alone will not solve the problem because they always come 'from outside' or 'from above'. For decades now experts have studied the problems of small farmers, tenants and farm-workers. But those affected by the problem have until now only had very limited chances to state their own views and make their own decisions. In spite of all efforts they have remained the object of development endeavours instead of becoming the principal agents for development.

Wealth and power are not only measured in material terms but also show themselves in the ability to be articulate, to be able to push through one's own interests within a group and to settle conflicts. All these should be prerequisites with which the lowest levels will be able to make use of the Comilla Project.

In 1972 the Asian regional conference of the FAO decided to give priority to development for the small farmers. The problems listed above are to be given special attention. In Indonesia, Nepal, Sri Lanka, India and Bangladesh, field workshops have been established in which small farmers and tenants will cooperate with development experts, civil servants of all levels, professors, development workers etc.

The discussion in working groups will be supplemented with specific talks in the villages. As a result people will not be talking *about* the small farmers but *with* the small farmers. The problem of communication will by no means be solved in this way, but it is a beginning which is already leading to new experiments. And for this Comilla is a key model.

One result is the view that basic groups of small farmers and tenants must grow up below the level of the cooperatives and village councils. Such groups cannot be built up from above through projects. Private groups and organisations must undertake this work, which should follow existing tendencies. So it is not a question of doing something for the small farmers but helping them to do it for themselves. The different regional meetings have produced suggestions for testing new methods and procedures in micro-projects in several disciplines.

The Philippines

At the beginning of 1974 a consumer cooperative opened a shop in Barrio Banadero in Batangas Province in the Philippines. It is not much more than a kiosk. Starting capital was 4,000 pesos and was raised by the selling of share certificates. By the beginning of August the capital had already risen to 25,000 pesos. But membership is not acquired just through the purchase of share certificates. Attendance at a training weekend is another condition of entry. Whoever wishes to take part brings along a sack of rice for his own food supply. During the weekend he learns not only how a cooperative operates but at the same time is made to understand how the cooperative can be used as a weapon in the struggle for social equality. Already two thousand members have been trained in this way in Batangas Province, and they have set up consumer cooperatives in sixteen villages.

The group of young men and women who are responsible for the shop in Barrio Banadero want as their next step to get rid of the middlemen. The latter dominate the local market by buying up rice after the harvest at the lowest prices. When rice becomes scarcer, they sell it at great profit.

Whoever wants to take up the fight against these middlemen must have his own storage facilities.

A cooperative in Pampanaga Province has managed to do just this. But this group faces other problems. With irrigation it would be possible to have two harvests a year. After the rice harvest, vegetables and water-melons could be planted and up to 10,000 pesos per hectare could be earned. Underground water is available and the cooperative has already bought the technical equipment for a tube-well. But it cannot be installed because a big landowner will not allow the water to be taken across his property.

In a Barrio in Nueva Ecija Province the farmers take their guests to see a piece of ground six hundred metres square, which their cooperative has bought. 'Here is where our storehouse will be built. We just have to wait until we have collected the means to go ahead. Later we shall also build our own rice mill, so that we can be independent of the middlemen.' They do not ask if it would be possible to receive help from abroad but trust in their own strength. The future appears as a common goal that can be achieved. All these groups belong to the Free Farmers Cooperative.

Thirteen thousand members in thirty-five provinces have formed with their families the Free Farmers Cooperative Inc (FFCI). It was founded in 1965 as the economic arm of the Federation of Free Farmers (FFF). Its most important projects are consumer cooperatives, credit unions, building and running storehouses and general organisation of the buying of rice, maize, copra, coffee, ginger etc. In some groups members have pooled their land for common cultivation. In addition there is common use of tractors, pumps and lorries.

The cooperatives are based on the ideological principles of the Federation of Free Farmers which was founded in 1953 and today has a membership of about 200,000 tenants, farmers, fishermen and agricultural workers. The chief founder and until today the inspiring personality in the Federation is Jeremias Montemayor. The movement considers the realisation of social equality to be the most fundamental and urgent problem in the Philippines. Less than 5 per cent

162

of the population account for over 65 per cent of the national income, while the other 95 per cent of the population have to share out the remaining 35 per cent of the income. The monopoly of power lies in the hands of the thin upper layer of large landowners and industrialists.

Seventy per cent of the population is engaged in agriculture, most of them as the tenants of big landowners. The Federation of Free Farmers thinks the only way to improve their lot is by land reform. (Present land transfer reform only includes regions cultivated with rice, maize and wheat. Sugar and coconut plantations which have caused the biggest social problems are not included.) It tries to influence legislation at government level and at grass roots level keeps up the pressure for implementing this legislation by giving its members legal assistance. Many farmers have several simultaneous law cases pending against their landlords. There are thirty-four lawyers working full time for the movement. The more simple types of case are taken over by members of the Federation who are not trained lawyers but have gained the necessary knowledge through long experience.

The Declaration of Principles of the Federation of Free Farmers sets out what are considered to be the most effective and lasting ways to bring about a reform of the power structures. The Federation feels that reform should be carried out by the tenants and workers educating and organising *themselves*, and in this way gaining their own social, economic and political power. The movement does not consider the only alternative to be force or passivity, but has chosen as a third way — the method of 'social organisation'. This cannot be arranged from the outside for the farmers but has to be accomplished by the farmers themselves.

Social equality takes absolute priority in all spheres. On this account philosophical and ideological education (which is based on the main points in the social teaching of the Catholic Church) plays an important role in the training of the basic groups right up to the education of the cadres. The movement has worked out its own theological foundations.

163

'Our official church is a church of the big landowners. It has no answer to the farmers' questions over the meaning of existence', claims the leader of the Ethics and Religion section of the Federation, who is still a farmer but does not hesitate to get into discussion with bishops and theologians.

The school programme is supplemented at all levels with courses which facilitate technical and organisational knowledge. The school courses are so arranged that the movement is able to train its cadres itself, from the basic level upwards. Even in the leadership, it is not specialists with university degrees who head the various departments but real representatives of the farmers, who understand the problems of the underprivileged rural population from their own experience. But even the Federation of Free Farmers is not spared the usual crises of growth. It is trying to solve the problem by decentralising power and decision-making authority.

China

China is about the same size as India. Yet it supports — without famine or starvation and only rarely resorting to food imports — a population half as big again. That alone is a measure of its achievement.

The Chinese agricultural system, as everyone knows, is rooted in the commune. It is important, however, to understand how the system evolved because communes, as they are known today, were not introduced until 1958.

The first priority of the Chinese communists when they came to power in 1949 was to end the feudal system of agriculture. Land reform began immediately after the Revolution and was a practical step towards mobilising the peasantry and gaining their political support. Until 1949 over 70 per cent of the farming area in China was in the hands of landlords and the rich peasantry. This land was redistributed to the poorer peasants and the landless. The process of land reform was supervised at the village level and it was completed in a very short time, though possibly with a good deal of bloodshed in the process.[7]

164

During the 1950s the transition to a cooperative farming system began to take place. The government was aware that the Chinese landscape could not change overnight from feudalism to collectivism. Instead the change was carried out in stages, the first priority being that the peasants were no longer tied to their landlords.

Between 1949 and 1952, in an attempt to minimise the deficiencies of farm units that were often too small to be economic, Mutual Aid Teams were introduced. A few families would pool their limited resources together and thereby make more efficient use of their land and labour. In the mid-1950s these were superseded by Advance Producers Cooperatives, which consisted of several villages amalgamated into a single economic unit. These proved too small to deal with the economic and administrative functions of a region and so in 1958 the commune system was established.

The communes are both the highest unit of agricultural organisation and the lowest unit of government. The area of most communes coincides with the Hsiang or former county. The communes are responsible for a region's political, administrative and organisational functions. They are a means of mobilising the latent productivity of the previously underemployed rural masses of China. The total land area of a commune varies from about three to twelve thousand hectares and the population from four to six thousand families. The Chinese estimate that there are about 76,000 communes.

Each commune has a tiered structure. At the top is the commune itself. This is subdivided into production brigades, consisting of a number of neighbouring villages. At the lowest level is the production team, organised for each village. Farming operations and the planning of agriculture are basically controlled by the brigades and production teams. Economic incentives are built into the communal system. Different kinds of activities, whether agricultural or industrial, earn 'work points' and a man's wage (paid in kind and cash) depends on the total work points earned in a month. However the rate at which work points are paid is related to the total income of the commune. So there are both individual and communal incentives. It is one of Mao's most fundamental injunctions that every advance in production should be reflected in improvement in the peasants' incomes.

After each harvest, each team reviews the year's output and assesses the level of the next year's production. Proposals for next year's investment go to the commune, which reviews them and then passes them on to the province. At the provincial level the plans for resource allocation, for example the need for seeds or an irrigation dyke, are discussed. A provincial plan is produced and each unit within that extended area is given its production target. Each province is expected to fulfil its plan, weather permitting.

The policy of self-reliance for each commune is in direct conflict with the policy of redistribution of incomes. Naturally some communes, with more fertile soils or a larger area, have a higher income than less well-endowed communes. Richer communes are taxed to help their poorer counterparts but the inequality in incomes is a problem which the Chinese have not yet completely overcome.[8]

Private ownership was not totally abolished and even now there is a residual private sector. Most families own their houses plus a plot of land on which they grow food for their own purposes and raise pigs and chickens. One tenth of all cultivated land in the commune is privately owned.

The transformation of the Chinese countryside into a collective system has not been an easy process. Between 1958 and 1963, during the Great Leap Forward, the new commune system functioned with a great deal of chaos and confusion.[9] Inadequate planning and mismanagement of resources, plus three successive years of drought and poor harvests, put great strains on the viability of the commune. Between 1960 and the early 1970s, very little official information about China's economic performance was available, but it seems evident that there was tremendous instability which set back the rate of productivity a good deal.

Investment in agriculture in the 1950s was poor and it

was only after stability returned in 1962 that the government recognised the very vital need to give more assistance to rural areas. Before 1962 they had followed the Soviet trend towards investment in capital production rather than in agriculture. For the productivity of the countryside to increase, the farmers also had to reinvest more of their own income in farming. But this reinvestment performance has not been good enough and what capital the government spent on the rural areas was spread too thinly.

The real test of course is whether the system works — above all, does it feed, clothe and house all the population, for that is the dominant question in Asia today? Here China scores heavily. The average income in China appears to be, in terms of real purchasing power, two or three times higher than in India and Pakistan and 50 to 100 per cent higher than in Thailand, the Philippines or Indonesia.[10] Certainly the income disparities between social classes and regions are much greater elsewhere in Asia.

China has also cured the seemingly endemic Asian disease of high rural underemployment. When there is little labour needed in the fields, the surplus is channelled into construction projects such as building irrigation works, roads and local industrial workplaces. Irrigation and water control are vital factors in improving the reliability and quantity of farming output. In the years between 1951 and 1971, the proportion of irrigated land to the total arable land in China increased from 20 to 78 per cent. The largest irrigation programmes have been in the major river basins, but thousands of smaller schemes are scattered throughout the cultivable countryside. Mechanisation has not advanced as far as the government anticipated in their plans and favours the cash-cropping rather than subsistence areas. Subsistence agriculture still predominates in most areas and is likely to continue to do so until the food production rate remains constantly ahead of the population growth rate.

The land/population balance in China is an unfavourable one. Only some 12 per cent of the total area is cultivated, i.e. about 260 million acres, of which 95 per cent is within the eastern third of the country. To extend the cultivatable area is too expensive and difficult a task. At the moment each family has approximately one hectare to farm. The Chinese have laid great emphasis on cultivating more intensively the existing area, through improved fertiliser application and new varieties of seed and pesticides. The environment provides many hazards to farming, particularly the unreliability of rainfall, flooding and the prevalence of disease.

Harvests in China have steadily increased since 1969, although in bad years, such as 1959-1962 and in 1972, the shortfall in production had to be made up with imports. In 1974 it is estimated that the Chinese imported ten million tons of grain. But viewed over the whole period since 1949, agricultural production has kept pace with population growth. In 1949 the grain harvest was in the region of 140 million tons. In 1952 it exceeded 150 million tons and during the 1950s the annual rate of increase was about 3 per cent, which is high by Third World standards. In 1961 grain output was estimated at 162 million tons. By 1973 this had shot up to over 250 million tons. Over the period 1949 to 1973 grain output has risen by an average of 2.5 per cent a year.

The rural area of China is capable of feeding both itself and the urban population. It also supplies the industrial sector with raw materials, such as cotton and minerals, and in return the industrial sector supplies it with equipment and fertilisers needed for the land. Industry is decentralised in China, the aim being that each commune should be self-sufficient in its industrial products as well as in its food. All sorts of industries exist in the countryside, such as sugar-refining, milk powder plants, paper-mills, fertiliser plants etc.

China's experience has shown that institutional transformation is a prerequisite for technical transformation. The Green Revolution, which other Asian countries pursued in such haste in the 1960s in order to try to achieve self-sufficiency, is not an end in itself. Increased agricultural production is not just a function of increased technological inputs, it has social and political dimensions as well. The system of centralised control and the use of the commune as the lowest administrative level mean that new ideas and

168

technologies can be diffused throughout the system from top to bottom and vice versa. The socialisation of agriculture was essential for the diffusion of plans and for a working agricultural policy to succeed.

Although China has had various setbacks in bad years, looked at over the long run she has succeeded in driving off poverty and unemployment and has made remarkable strides towards a self-sufficient economy.

It seems we have a problem in three parts — today, tomorrow and the day after.

Today the outlook is grim, very grim. Grain stocks are minimal in the rich world, and the poor countries have no money to buy even the little that is available.

The outlook for tomorrow is mixed. On paper — as in chapter 8 — it all looks very possible. Given the will, the imagination and the resources it looks as if agricultural production could be raised quite significantly — at least enough to get on top of rising population.

But in reality the impediments are quite severe, not least the political arrangements that so dominate the Third World, political arrangements which favour a well-entrenched middle and upper class that fears any kind of change that comes from below.

We ought, then, to make it clear what the price of failure is. The FAO have estimated,[1] assuming a population growth of 2.7 per cent, that the demand for food in the developing countries will grow at an annual rate of 3.6 per cent. Over fifteen years this means an increase of some 70 per cent. Even this projection is a conservative one. Inevitably aggregated figures such as these conceal wide disparities between individual countries. In the Far East in particular and to a lesser extent in Africa, average per caput demand for calories, on this calculation, would remain below the level required for moderate human activity until well into the 1980s.

Set against this 3.6 per cent annual growth rate in demand is the actual trend in agricultural production. A Third World which by and large is not following the prescriptions of chapter 7 is expected to increase its production of food at only 2.9 per cent a year. This trend is based on an average of the output between 1961 and 1973 and then extrapolated.[2]

What this means — if these projections are continued through to 1985 — is that the developing countries will have an annual net cereal deficit of almost eighty-five million tons compared with a deficit of only sixteen million tons annual average in 1969-71. If the traditional cereal-exporting countries among the Third World countries are excluded the picture becomes worse. Then the projected cereal deficit jumps to around a hundred million tons a year. Even this is a conservative estimate. Bad weather conditions can raise deficits in a single year quite sharply. The cereal deficit in the bad 1973/74 season, excluding food exporting nations, was estimated at fifty-two million tons. (Sixty million tons if socialist developing countries are included). So a similar type of catastrophe in the 1980s might mean a shortfall of 120 million tons or more.

The cost of importing eighty-five million tons of cereals in 1985 — assuming it were available (the developed countries could probably grow it without too much difficulty) — would be at 1973/74 prices 17,500 million dollars a year. Even at 1969/72 prices it would cost 8,000 million dollars (at the moment expenditure on American food aid totals a mere 1.3 billion dollars). The Third World certainly cannot afford to buy that amount and is it possible in political terms to conceive of a jump in food aid thirteen-fold in just over a decade? It is most doubtful. In short the developing countries have no realistic alternative but to follow the prescriptions of chapter 7.

There is one other alternative: a world-wide depression of living standards and increasingly widespread malnutrition. There will of course be the occasional big famine — Sahel or Bihar style — but we are more likely to see a different kind of famine — famine thinly spread right across great chunks of the Third World, gradually, slowly, but definitely deepening its hold until nature begins to take its age old course of allowing deaths to rise in order to match the realities of the situation.

So now we have looked at today and found that is gloomy. We have looked at tomorrow and seen a little hope, though with disaster not far away.

For the sake of rubbing home our argument, however, we should look at the day after tomorrow. And this we do on the assumption that our suggested policies have failed. We assume, in the face of all the evidence, that the rich countries continue to bail out the poor countries with their food surplus between now and 1985. In this case[3] we will be faced with a Third World population of around 2.5 thousand million[4] as compared with the 1.5 thousand million twenty years earlier.

If population continued to grow from this base at 2.5 per cent a year (the present Asian growth figure) the rural population of Asia alone would, by the year AD 2020, be 1.3 thousand million. (This figure assumes the non-agricultural population increases at 3.8 per cent a year — itself a dangerous presumption given the mounting urban problems we examined in chapter 6.) The total Asian population would reach 2.1 thousand million by AD 2000.

With growth rates like this it is unlikely that technological progress could cope. However before we examine the evidence behind this pessimistic conclusion we ought in fairness to summarise the viewpoint of Walter Pawley, who recently retired as Director of the Policy Advisory Bureau in FAO. He has argued that if thirty-six thousand million people had to be fed by the year 2070 it could be done. And that it could be done without recourse to synthetic food.

He believes this requires two major technical breakthroughs, both of which are within the bounds of possibility. First, techniques for the continuous cultivation of the soil in the humid tropics after the tree cover has been removed. This, he argues, would make the seven million square kilometres of the Amazon basin and a smaller area of equatorial Africa available for intensive farming.

The second breakthrough would be a way of desalinating sea water at costs low enough to be economic for irrigation and with sources of electricity cheap enough to pump the water long distances and up considerable heights.

This breakthrough, well within man's ingenuity, would turn the deserts of the world into great granaries. The Sahara alone would add twelve million square kilometres to the world's cultivable area — an area almost equal to the total

172

cultivated land in the world today.

Irrigation of this kind would also make it possible to provide perennial irrigation to easily cultivable lands, to the vast areas under permanent pasture and to the lands now under tropical forests.

What these technological advances mean is simply this: that instead of fourteen million square kilometres of land surface (one tenth of the earth's surface) being cultivable, seventy million square kilometres would be. Only the mountains too rugged and lofty for cultivation and the one fifth of the earth under permanent ice or snow, or in the permafrost zone, would remain uncultivable.

This leaves the world with 56 million square kilometres of unutilised but potentially cultivable land. Half of this would be in warm temperate climates. With perennial irrigation three crops a year could be grown. If yields average only twice those now obtained in Europe (a modest assumption given a hundred years of technical progress) total food output could be raised to thirty times what it is today. And if yields could be increased by 4 per cent food production would increase fifty-fold.

It is not that we do not accept Walter Pawley's prognosis of the technical feasibility of feeding thirty-six million people. Theoretically it is perhaps possible. In practice the people are in the wrong place — in Asia, not in the 'new granary' of the Sahara. We have to deal with the situation that arises where the people are:

Briefly here are the reasons for our longterm pessimism.

Fertiliser, for all its success in raising yields dramatically, appears to have its limits. As increasing amounts of fertiliser are used the gain in yields diminishes rapidly. In the developed countries farmers are only getting five pounds of extra grain out of each additional pound of fertiliser used. By contrast farmers in poor countries can easily obtain ten to twelve pounds of grain for every pound of fertiliser.

Table 23 shows this phenomenon of diminishing returns in Iowa, the corn state of America. But fertiliser application is not a straightforward question of greater input producing

173

greater yields. The crop response to fertilisers is influenced by the nature of the soil, its nutrient deficiency, the type of seed used, the availability of water etc. Soil surveys are virtually unheard of in developing countries and farmers are unlikely to know exactly what proportion of nitrogen, phosphorus or potassium to put on their fields.

Once farmers begin to use fertilisers they need to continue application throughout the growth cycle of each crop. The next year they will need a little more fertiliser in order to

Table 23: A typical fertiliser response curve: corn yield response to fertiliser in Iowa, 1964 (Source: US Department of Agriculture)

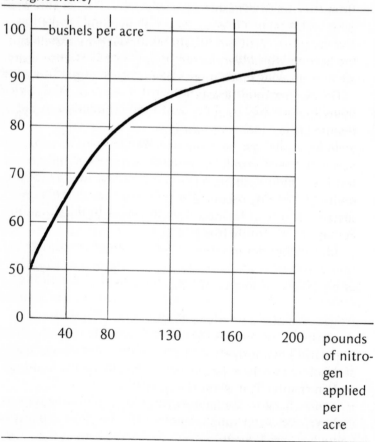

sustain the yield. Since prices have risen so dramatically since 1973, far fewer farmers can afford the correct supply quantities in order to maintain a profit margin. Instead of the environmental risks that they were formerely accustomed to, farmers are now faced with economic risks which are in many respects much harder to bear.

Next there is the question of yields. As farmers move up the curve of yield per acre a point of diminishing returns is eventually reached at which additional costs begin to exceed additional returns. In the United States raising the average corn yields from ninety to a hundred bushels an acre requires far more fertiliser than is needed to raise yields from fifty to sixty bushels. Japan's rice yields, despite her great technical proficiency, have only doubled in the last seventy years. Yields in Britain that, under the stimulus of the Second World War, increased two-fold in twenty years are now growing much more slowly.

Developing countries start from a much lower base and there is enormous room for improvement. But greater yields require greater inputs of nutrients and water. Dramatic yield increases have been obtained in limited areas where new varieties of seed have been planted with the necessary fertilisers and irrigation. Yields have also increased where multiple-cropping occurs. But these yields are difficult to sustain because of financial and environmental hazards. Perhaps in the future it would be more worthwhile to discuss yield increases not in terms of quantity but of quality. Improved yields would imply a greater output of calories or protein from an area of land.

Irrigation is also a problem. The world's rivers offer diminishing possibilities. The irrigation potential of most of the world's major rivers, — the Nile, Yellow, Indus, Ganges and Colorado — have largely been realised. But as we have seen in chapter 7, it is not the large schemes which are the most beneficial to the farmers. The scope for irrigation from underground water supplies and dams on small streams is still underdeveloped. Further expansion of these small schemes,

175

which are geographically dispersed and relatively inexpensive, is certainly possible in many parts of the developing world. In India alone the number of electric and diesel pumps rose from under one million in 1966 to over 2.7 million in 1972. The number of private tube-wells rose from 113,000 to 550,000 over the same period. Similarly there is need for research into how to conserve water and re-use waste water, how to reduce evaporation loss and minimise seepage. All these measures would enable farmers to make a better use of existing supplies.

The seas, it is increasingly argued, will replenish man's feeding bowl. Here is a great source of untapped potential, merely waiting relatively inexpensive breakthroughs in technology. But in fact the limits of the world's fisheries are already being reached. Japan and the USSR are at the forefront of the fishing industry and have developed new and expensive technologies, such as electronically controlled detector devices and factories aboard ships. But pollution of coastal waters and exhaustion of supply have led them further and further afield into the relatively untapped areas of the South Atlantic and Indian Oceans.

In 1955 the world's catch was twenty-eight million tons. By 1970 this had risen to sixty-nine million tons, which represents a very rapid annual growth. However since 1970 the rate of increase has slowed down considerably. Many experts now argue that we have approached the limits of edible fish production.

One of the biggest barriers to improving the protein content of diets in developing countries is not that the fish are not there to be caught, but that once they are caught the developed countries take the bulk of the catch. Peru is the world's biggest supplier of fish. Its catch could raise nutritional standards in Latin America to those of southern Europeans. Instead 95 per cent of this protein source is exported and used as animal foodstuff. These animals then become the source of the rich man's extravagant protein.[5]

There will undoubtedly be great strides forward in the

technology of food producing. For example it is likely that before long there will be a strain of wheat with a 25 per cent higher protein content than is usual today. In the United States experiments are being carried out to change completely the composition of vegetable proteins in cereals. For instance a hybrid maize has been developed which has a nutritional value 70 per cent higher than normal.

Yeast is now being used as a means of converting petroleum derivatives and organic wastes into edible forms of protein known as single-cell protein. Yeast can be used as an additive in foods, such as soups and sausages.

Revolutions in protein supply from non-conventional sources tend to be developed in the West and for the West. They rely on expensive technologies and costly inputs. The oil crisis has vastly increased the price of petroleum-derived protein and it is unlikely to be of commercial use in feeding the fast-expanding hungry world. But technical advances have been made in improving the yields of conventional foods in developing countries. The best opportunities lie in crops which are already grown in the developing countries, cottonseed, peanuts and soya-beans for example. These crops have a high protein content and could be converted into attractive protein foods. All the world's oilseed cakes contain more protein than the total catch of edible fish, enough to double the protein consumptions of developing countries.[6] At present these oilseed cakes are used to feed cattle, but with further research they could be used as human food.

Throughout the world there are several research centres, each with responsibility for selected crops. The aim of these centres is to develop new or crossed strains of local crops which produce greater yields and have a higher nutrient value than the original varieties. For instance researchers at the International Institute for Tropical Agriculture at Ibadan, Nigeria, have produced crosses in legumens which successfully yield a third more than the local variety. At the same time they only need two applications of pesticide a season instead of ten.[7]

Technological breakthroughs in increasing the yields of

tropical crops are occurring all the time. In many cases the added cost is not beyond the reach of peasant farmers. But technical feasibility and the organisational capacity of each country to make use of new technologies do not always go together. There are certain bottlenecks in adopting new technologies, the principal one being the lack of incentive to innovate. If there is a price incentive to innovate and sufficient extension work to encourage farmers to adopt new methods, then the demand for improved technologies will grow and their advantages will be realised.

Increasingly scholars are arguing that what has happened in the Sahel is an early warning signal of a significant change in the earth's climate.

Climatological data show that the earth's temperature rose by one degree Fahrenheit (0.4 degrees Centigrade) between 1880 and 1940. Since 1940, however, it has dropped by 0.5 degrees Fahrenheit. Lester Brown observes :

> No one can say whether this observed temperature decline in the past 25 years was due to long-term natural cyclical changes, to increased particulate matter in the upper atmosphere from volcanic activity, to the expansion of agricultural dustbowls in parts of Africa and Asia, to expanding industrial activity, or to some factor not yet observed. What is significant is that climatologists do agree that man's activities are now on a scale that can affect, and may already be affecting the earth's climate.[8]

Dr Reid Bryson, Director of the Institute for Environmental Studies at the University of Wisconsin, and Hubert Lamb, an eminent British meteorologist, take a very pessimistic line. The key to climatic stability is the balance of radiation from the sun. Since there has been reduced radiation input in the past thirty-five years, excessively low temperatures have been recorded at the poles. The result has been a southward displacement of the major climatic belts in the northern hemisphere. Bryson and Lamb argue that the monsoon belt is shifting gradually south. This is the major factor behind the recent prolonged drought in the Sahara. It is also, they believe, going to reduce rainfall in the Indian subcontinent and South-East Asia.

Other authorities see the Sahel drought as a short-term phenomenon.[9] Between 1950 and 1965 the rainfall in West Africa was good and newly independent governments encouraged the nomads to increase their livestock and extend the grazing area. The result has been overgrazing which has caused a deterioration of the local climate. Albedo — reflection from the earth's surface — has increased on the bare land and so local temperatures have risen. Wind erosion is encouraged and the desert tends to spread. The situation can be stabilised by increasing the vegetation cover and allowing the system to establish its old equilibrium.

The Central Intelligence Agency has recently published a report which analyses the implications of long-term climatic changes on world food production.[10] If the earth's surface does cool considerably by the end of this century, countries at the northern and southern extremes and those nearest the equator will suffer enormous cutbacks in their agricultural output. Countries in mid-latitudes will be least disrupted by frost or drought. The United States and Argentina will be the only major grain areas not to be affected. The CIA is the first to recognise the enormous social, economic and political implications of this: the United States will have complete power to choose which country should receive assistance and would thus be able to dictate the fate of millions in the developing world.

Both the pessimistic and optimistic climatologists are basing their theories of trends on limited evidence. It remains to be seen what the future climate holds in store for the world's population, but the long-term assessment is hardly encouraging. One wonders, given these formidable barriers, if optimism about the long term is only delusion. Better to get the house in order now than to test one's luck.

Round about 3,844 years ago, Joseph successfully interpreted Pharaoh's dream of the 'seven kine'. And in return Pharaoh put Joseph, with his great organising ability, in charge of Egypt's anti-famine campaign; the devastation of an empire was averted.

Many at the World Food Conference held in Rome in November 1974 expected Dr Henry Kissinger to play the role of the latter-day Joseph. Thirteen months before when he asked for this emergency UN Conference, there was a feeling that he had perceived what his fellow politicians had not — that the world was on the edge of the greatest famine in its history and, if it were to be averted, some pretty drastic decisions would have to be taken.

But we misjudged Dr Kissinger. He did come to the Conference in person but entered the hall a bare minute before he spoke and left for Cairo immediately afterwards. His speech was as skimpy as his visit. No great new initiatives were taken. No new vision was spelt out. Perhaps Kissinger, who apparently only had time for two hours' sleep the night before his speech, had had no time to dream.

The Russians, who with the Americans must take a large share of the blame for the present shortage of food in the world marketplace, disgusted many of the delegates with simplistic notions of how the world could feed twelve times its present population. They seem to forget that the Sahara and the Amazon — the futurists' granaries of tomorrow — are thousands of miles away from the majority of hungry people. And that people want to grow their own food, not live for ever on someone else's surplus.

The Chinese, whose speech was awaited with great anticipation, were equally disappointing. The Conference hall had filled up to capacity. Would the Chinese — the one large country in Asia that knew how to feed itself — have

180

some answers? But it was a dull speech, full of attacks on the two superpowers, America and Russia, and containing only a boring, unpassionate appeal to follow the Chinese way.

But it was the British who made the most insensitive contribution. The Minister of Agriculture, Fred Peart, apparently oblivious of the crisis at hand, spoke of his worry of increasing malnutrition in Britain and went on to tell his press conference that he wanted the British to eat more.

In this kind of atmosphere it was not surprising that no great decisions were taken, no historic initiatives made. Instead, the Conference lumbered on with delegates staying up late in the evening to change commas and full stops in resolutions that no one is ever likely to read, much less take notice of.

There were three principal issues with which the Conference was supposed to be grappling. First, the short-term crisis — the time between then and the next harvest when millions of people, maybe tens of millions, were likely to die and hundreds of millions find their level of nutrition severely and painfully reduced, unless emergency relief were forthcoming.

1975 became a critical year. At the time of writing it is difficult to estimate just how many millions have actually died. We do know, however, that all over the Third World people have cut back on the food they consume. And over time this is bound to lead to increased malnutrition and a subsequent increase in rates of mortality. Death rates have gone up in a dozen and maybe as many as twenty countries.

Surprisingly there was no real debate on just how severe the crisis was — that seemed to be taken as read. At the most there was some quibbling from the Americans on whether the FAO's estimate of an immediate need for 9.5 million tons of grain was on the high side. But even they admitted that the shortfall was seven to eight million tons and that this estimate was based on a very conservative interpretation of what hunger meant. Some experts for example advocated the year 1971 — the last good year — as a benchmark. Work out the deficit, they said, by measuring the fall in nutrition levels from that year. The chief American economist in the delegation, Dr Paarlburg, admitted that this would probably give a much higher figure than 9.5 million tons, but he thought it politically unrealistic to discuss the crisis in those terms.

Yet although there was no debate on the substances of the matter — the need for imperative action if crises and catastrophe were to be averted — there was an enormous divergence of opinion on who should pay. The American delegation argued that if they were to give their fair share of the 9.5 million tons, this meant that they would have to find 5 million, the Canadians 1 million, the EEC 2.5 million, and Australia and others 1 million. And since they had no reserves to speak of, this would mean restricting some of their already agreed commercial exports, re-evaluating the stocks they needed to carry for their own strategic reserves and then finally reducing the amount of grain going to their own livestock. They argued that if this were done, they would run into enormous political and economic difficulties. First, inflation would be exacerbated as the government stepped into the market-place to buy up grain. Second, it would require Congress to approve a sizable budgetary appropriation. And in a time of economic stringency this was just not on.

A group of prominent senators who were on hand — Hubert Humphrey and George McGovern in particular — took the leader of the delegation, the Secretary of Agriculture, Earl Butz, publicly to task on this. 'One less Trident submarine', said Humphrey, 'and you have the money we need.' Such was the emotional atmosphere at the Conference that the senators persuaded Butz to fire off a telegram to the White House asking for an immediate commitment to one million tons. But the answer came back 'No'. A senior member of the American delegation volunteered the opinion that if the oil-rich countries paid for the grain, then the proposal could be sold to the American public despite the inflationary consequences.

The 'Arabs should pay' refrain was one of the more unpleasant features of the Conference. It had been started by

Kissinger in his opening remarks and continued by almost every western delegate. (To everyone's surprise, Cuba argued the same point.) But it was transparently a counter-productive ploy. For a start, the oil-rich countries have only had this new-found surplus for a couple of years — and the old rich never spent it on the poor when they had it. But more important was the unacknowledged fact that the new rich are beginning to send large amounts of funds to help the poorer countries. Iran is spending 7 per cent of its GNP a year on foreign aid compared with the western average of 0.35 per cent. Saudi Arabia is increasingly channelling its funds into the World Bank and other development agencies. If the western nations are serious about encouraging the OPEC countries to spend their new-found wealth in the developing world, they will have to stop this kind of hectoring attack. It is not fair to the facts. And psychologically it is bound to produce resistance.

The only western country which actually gave a lead on the key question of reducing consumption was Norway. A new policy, which began to be introduced in July 1974, increased the cost of animal feed above its market price. The intention is to shift emphasis away from the type of meat production requiring a lot of feed grains. In addition the price of meat which is not produced with feed grains was made relatively cheaper. Norway also attempted unsuccessfully to persuade the Conference to adopt a resolution declaring that 'the diet of the developed countries should not be taken as a model of a satisfactory state of nutrition.'

As it turned out, the 1974-75 situation was salvaged by a remarkable coincidence of forces.

Most important was the impact of the recession in the United States. 'The demand for grain for livestock feeding is 29,000,000 tons down on 1974', explained Mr Richard Bell, the Department of Agriculture official in charge of foreign assistance. 'Americans are cutting back on their meat in a way we ourselves never anticipated. Less pork is being produced now than at any time in the past 30 years.' This was a major influence in bringing the price of wheat down from 5.08 dollars a bushel in November 1974 to around

3.78 dollars in March 1975. Mr Jim Placke, the senior state department official who monitors the crisis for Dr Kissinger, commented: 'The shortage of stocks is just not being reflected in the market today. The price fall is amazing given the fact we have no stocks.'

The effect of this fall in grain prices was two-fold. First it enabled needy importing countries who buy grain commercially to get more for their money than anticipated. Second, it gave a big boost to the food aid programmes of western countries which by and large were established in terms of financial appropriation rather than quantity.

The Americans, who spent 1.6 billion dollars on food aid during the financial year 1974-75, were able to buy as much as 3,750,000 tons more than was originally estimated. The decision, however, to increase food aid from 891 million to 1.6 billion dollars — made possible by domestic pressure from concerned citizens — was delayed for weeks while Dr Kissinger wrestled tortuously with Congress about the definition of food aid. Dr Kissinger wanted a flexible interpretation so that he could give food not just to meet humanitarian needs but as a form of budgetary support to Chile, Jordan, Egypt and South Vietnam.

The other major surprise development was the increase in commercial buying of food grains by India. By general consent India was the biggest problem although not the most intractable (that was reserved for Bangladesh). India did this partly because of the concessional financing of her oil imports arranged by a number of OPEC countries and because the windfall profits from her sizable sugar exports eased her always chronic balance of payments problem — and partly because national pride dictated that India must avoid at all cost becoming dependent once again on American handouts.

1975, however, was certainly better than 1974. The monsoon in Asia began on time. In the Sahel there was rain. And the US harvest was a record.

The food aid situation dramatically improved — of that there is no doubt. In 1975, well ahead of the critical period of shortage, the grain exporting countries of the West began

184

to make the right decisions: by August the White House had already budgeted 1.3 billion dollars for food aid — almost double what they had allocated at the same time the year before. Moreover, the United States did not bear any longer the burden of having to give food as a kind of political support to Laos, South Vietnam and Cambodia. This tied up 17 per cent of 1974's food total.

Australia and Canada have also become more generous. After the World Food Council meeting in June 1975 the grain exporters only fell one million tons short of the council's target of ten million tons of grain. The major culprit was the EEC, which stubbornly refused to do its bit.

In sum, the difference between 1974 and 1975 was enormous.

But for all this the situation was still extremely grave. Even with a good harvest, the developing countries needed to import at least forty million tons of grain. The extra food aid helped but still 75 per cent of their needs had to be paid for by purchases on the open market — the same market the Russians were buying in..1974 and 1975 prices for oil and food wiped out the financial reserves of many developing countries. The International Monetary Fund estimates that the balance-of-payments deficits for non-oil-exporting developing countries was 36 billion dollars in 1975 compared with 27 billion dollars a year before. The 1974 figure itself was three times larger than the 1973 one.

Moreover, the commodity boom of 1973 which did much to bail the developing countries out of the 1974 debacle is now over. In the two years there has been a sharp downward turn in their terms of trade. The poor countries are earning less even though they are working as hard, or even harder, than they were three years ago. This brings us to the Russians and what they do or are allowed to do is critically important. The 1975 Russian harvest was estimated to face a shortfall of 33 millions tons. If the Russians were allowed to purchase all they wanted, wheat prices could shoot up way over last year's record high of 5 dollars a ton, a price that developing countries just cannot afford. Compare this with the 1972 price of 1.80 dollars, a price which had remained constant for some years. It is not surprising that the United States is chided for its hypocrisy. Last year the United States gained more from the rise in food prices than it lost from the rise in oil prices.

After a great deal of haggling — and an initial moratorium on sales — the Russians are going to be allowed to be regular buyers in the United States grain market. And in return for this the Russians will buy in a less tentative and disruptive way than they have done in the past. At the very least they will be buying five million tons a year — and given the likely deterioration of weather in Russian latitudes it could well be much more than that. But this should not happen. The rich must not export grain to their fellow rich while others are starving. The developing countries should be allowed into the marketplace first — so they can shop at a price they can more easily afford. Only then should the Russians be given the green light. This may require the complicated step of creating a two-tier market for grain sales. But that is not beyond the wit of man to devise. And of course, if this were done, Canada, Australia and the EEC would have to come to some arrangements to share the burden with the United States.

The second point of discussion at the Conference was how to build up an international system of reserves so that when the harvest fails again — as undoubtedly it will — we will not be as unprepared as we are now. In his speech Dr Kissinger had called for a world-wide system of food reserves of sixty million tons above present carry-over levels. In the end the rich countries agreed to try to work out a system to set aside ten million tons a year. Assuming there is good weather in the next few years, this could be regarded as an adequate start. But on the more likely assumption of variable weather, if not bad weather, together with rising population trends, it is manifestly inadequate. After all, the United States alone averaged food aid of nine million tons annually between 1968 and 1972. And even for the ten million target, there was no agreement on who should hold the reserves and who should pay for them. The conference Secretariat's proposal for an internationally held stock of half a million tons to meet extraordinary emergencies was not even discussed.

The policy of holding stocks in private traders' hands, as advocated by Earl Butz, is very shortsighted indeed. For something so crucial and sensitive as food, there must be government intervention, control and subsidy. Otherwise, in a time of crisis, food will end up in the stomachs of the highest bidders.

However, we must note two words of caution on the question of government-held stocks. If stocks are to be rebuilt, the mistakes in the use of surpluses in the 1960s must not be repeated — bailing out poor countries to the point where they have no incentive to be self-reliant. Too often poor countries made the decision to forget about food, safe in the knowledge that the American Food for Peace Programme would always be there, and to concentrate their resources on other aspects of the economy — or even their armies. It also produced in some countries an unhealthy psychological dependency. Food aid, then, must be carefully controlled. It can for example be used as payment in kind to unemployed workers hired to develop the agricultural infrastructure — building irrigation and drainage channels, anti-erosion contour furrows, tree planting etc. It should be pointed out however that there is a danger that such rural works programmes will be yet another step in the direction of developing an infrastructure that favours the richer farmers (see the discussion in chapters 7 and 8).

Second, food aid must not be used as a political weapon. As one wag has said, 'The Arabs have crude, but the Americans have food.' And it is true that the Americans in particular now have an enormous political weapon in their hands. The omens are not too good either, for in 1974 80 per cent of American food aid was going to America's allies in South-East Asia. And two-thirds of the fertiliser purchased by the US government in 1974 for overseas assistance went to South Vietnam.

The other medium-term issue was the vexed question of fertilisers. The developing countries consume about 15 per cent of the world's production of eighty-four million tons of nutrients. They only produce about 7 per cent themselves: the balance has to be imported. In 1973/74 it cost them 1.6 billion dollars to meet the gap. In 1975 price rises pushed that figure close to 5.5 billion dollars. The FAO reckon that the twenty-one most seriously affected Third World countries faced a fertiliser shortfall of at least 1,800,000 tons in 1975. Commitments to subsidised schemes run by the FAO totalled at the beginning of the Conference 80,000 tons. Israel had pledged 50,000 tons; Holland 12,000; Norway 9,000; and Britain 2,500. During the Conference Japan offered 25,000 and Kuwait 2,500 tons.

So much for the medium term. The final key aim of discussion of the Conference was long-term agricultural improvement. The World Bank has estimated the hard-core poor of the Third World numbers seven hundred million small farmers, share-croppers and landless peasants. Two-thirds live in only four countries — India, Indonesia, Bangladesh and Pakistan; 19 per cent are in Africa and 13 per cent in Latin America and the Caribbean. These are the people with an annual income of 50 dollars or less whose lives are most threatened by the squeeze between population growth and agricultural output.

The Bank has calculated that the cost of getting the rural poor on the road to an annual 5 per cent growth in production is 80 dollars a head — a global cost of little more than 100 billion dollars over ten years. Not much when compared with the projected 170 billion dollars total investment, public and private, in developing countries in 1974, but quite a lot when measured against the total annual investment of the lower-income countries where the poor are concentrated — a mere 25 billion dollars in their case.

Yet despite all the evidence that, if the resources were forthcoming, perpetual world food crises, each one worse than the last, could be avoided, no rich country was prepared publicly to make new and significant commitments. Instead, the Conference agreed to establish a World Food Council and a Special Agricultural Fund. The former is meant to be a high-powered ministerial level watchdog and the latter the collecting-plate for a great new surge in giving. Both are still in their early stages of preparation. However the omens are good, particularly with the latter.

The World Food Conference, it seems, did not live up to all

the expectations many had for it. Yet progress was definitely made. Moreover the conference put the issue of food on the political map. Readers of *Le Monde, The Times,* the *New York Times, Tages Anzeiger* — and the *Mid-Western Farmers Weekly* — now know that there is a serious situation. And that is an important first step.

Yet when all is said and done, the Third World itself has to choose its own model of development. Of course free choice is made more difficult, given all the outside pressures that bear in on them. But they are not insuperable. Given the will profound changes in political direction can be taken. So the question is: which direction?

Increasingly it is being said at the highest levels of the developed establishment — in the FAO, the World Bank and the universities — that the Chinese have shown the way. They have given priority to people in the countryside, they have discouraged migration and rapid urbanisation, and by and large they have kept everyone adequately fed. And they have done this when population pressures were much more severe than they were in Japan, the other great success story, when she was developing.

Certainly there seems to be an argument for carefully examining what the Chinese have done and how they have done it. Yet we would advise caution. Most of those we have spoken to are careful to point out that it would be difficult to transpose a Chinese political system into another culture. 'Can one imagine the Italians adopting the British political system', said one expert 'much less the Indians adopting the Chinese?' It is true that looking at things from far off one can underestimate the vast differences that exist in cultural attitudes.

Remember too that our information on China is incomplete. We do not know what price in terms of human suffering and loss of individual freedom has been paid by the Chinese people for their economic and social success.

Another direction is the Tanzanian one. The *ujamaa* village idea depends much more on persuasion and incentive than the Chinese way. Yet we can see that progress is painfully slow. Tanzania, which does not have insufferable population pressures, can afford the luxury of time. Other countries, particularly those in Asia, cannot.

A third direction is suggested by the small-scale projects of Comilla, in Bangladesh, the Free Farmers in the Philippines and Glencolumbkille in Ireland. These projects, operating within fairly rigid and uninspired political systems, have built up, independent of government, a strong peasants' movement. They share the same idealism as does Tanzania, but they have already managed — perhaps because they have been going longer — to achieve some of the goals Tanzania seeks. Yet those who work in these projects would be the first to argue that, although they could always do with more financial resources, this has rarely been their prime bottleneck. It has been leadership — leadership that is prepared to work with peasant farmers at their own level, leadership which is not pompous, overbearing and remote; above all, leadership which has knowledge, dedication, commitment and vision.

It may well be that one of the most critical jobs is to use some of these models as training-grounds for future community leaders, so that the Comillas, Free Farmers and Glencolumbkilles can be multiplied a hundred-fold, a thousand-fold.

When there are enough projects of this kind in operation around the Third World, these minute particles of endeavour will begin to coagulate like globules of quicksilver — and at that point the change will become tangible and visible. Then a certain mood, tempo and spirit will have been established. This is revolution from below. Given the impossibility of another Chinese-style revolution — even if that is what is wanted — this is probably the only way to proceed.

There is, we are aware, a certain note of pessimism inherent in these conclusions. If China, for many understandable reasons, is unlikely to be carbon-copied around the Third World, Tanzania at the moment is still an idea — vaguely appealing, but lacking at present in sufficient substance to be widely emulated. If the Japanese way is taken to be part of the past, there is for its partisans the topical advantage of a modern-day repeat performance in Taiwan. But for all the doubts and reservations, the moral of the tale is clear and obvious — a way must be found quickly of turning the frontiers of the developing countries in the direction of the countryside. For that is where the root of the problem is to be found. Even if the model is to be an eclectic blend of China, Japan, Comilla, Taiwan, Glencolumbkille, Tanzania and World Bankism, nothing can move forward without the will to think anew. But first must come the will.

Acknowledgements and Notes

Acknowledgements

We wish to thank the many people who have made this book possible. First, the World Council of Churches, who commissioned from us the report on which this book is based. Second, our typists and translators. Third, all those in countries round the world who so freely gave us their time and knowledge and, finally, our families to whom this book is dedicated.

Out of all these people it is almost impossible to single out those who helped us most. But our gratitude is particularly reserved for Graeme Jackson, C.I. Itty, Sheila Ray, Steven Whittle, Hilda Gage, Gabrielle Merchez, Helder Camara, William Clark, Leif Christophersen, Keith Abercrombie, Sartaj Aziz, Barbara Ward, David Runnels, Gerry Montemayor, Alice Clark and Christoph Dickson.

And of course Anne, Carmen, Miriam, Carl, Rachel and Dominik.

Notes

2 The bottleneck

1 Lester R. Brown, *In the Human Interest,* New York, 1974, p160.

3 Why is there a food shortage today?

1 From *Population Bulletin,* 'Population and Affluence', 1974, p.4.
2 Second Report of the Club of Rome, Stuttgart, 1974. 'Menschheit am Wendepunkst' by Mihailo Mesapovic, Eduard Pestel, p.150.
3 CERES 42, 1974, p.32.
4 CERES 39, 1974, p.49.
5 Lyle P. Schertz, 'World Food: Prices and the Poor', *Foreign Affairs,* April 1974.
6 Cf. James Grant, 'Energy Shock and the Development Prospect' in *Agenda for Action 1974,* New York/Washington, p.31-32.
7 See Robert S. McNamara's speech to the governing body of the World Bank, 30 September 1974.
8 CERES 43, 1975, p.7.
9 CERES 38, 1964, p.56.
10 'Most US Fertilizer Aid said to be going to South Vietnam', *Herald Tribune,* 11 September 1974.
11 David R. Browe, 'See the Bottomless Norm of Plenty', *Development Forum,* March 1975, p.6.
12 John S. and Carol E. Steinhart, 'Energy Use in the US Food System', *Science,* vol.184, p.312 and 313.
13 Lawrence D. Hills, 'Making the Good Earth Feed your Children's Children', *Development Forum,* May 1975.
14 CERES 43, p.6.
15 PAN, the World Food Conference newspaper, 6 November 1974.
16 Lester R. Brown, 'The Need for a World Food Reserve', *Wall Street Journal,* 10 October 1973.
17 *The Limits to Growth,* London, 1972.
18 Lester R. Brown, *In the Human Interest,* p.22.
19 ibid.
20 ibid, p.26.
21 Gunnar Myrdal, *Asian Drama* (shortened by Seth S. King), London, 1972, p.275.
22 United Nations, Population Bulletin 7, 1963, p.144.
23 William Rich, *Smaller Families Through Social and Economic Progress,* Overseas Development Council, Washington, Monograph 7, p.9.

24 Quoted in J. Castro, *The Geopolitics of Hunger*, London, 1952, p.214.
25 CERES 42, 1974, p.7.

4 Hunger

1 Larry Minear, *New Hope for the Hungry*, New York, 1975, p.10.
2 CERES 43, p.14.
3 UNESCO *Courier*, 5/1975.
4 F.J. Raddatz, Weldernährungscrise, Hamburg, 1969, p.27.
5 *Far Eastern Economic Review*, 16, 1974; *Neue Zürcher Zeitung*, 28 February 1975.
6 Barbara Böttger, *700 Million without a future*, Hamburg, 1975, p.63.
7 Castro, op.cit., p.194.
8 UNESCO *Courier*, 5/1975, p.30.
9 CERES 38, 1974, p.30.
10 *Herald Tribune*, 4 November 1974.

5 From food aid to world food security

1 FAO Ad Hoc Consultation on World Food Security. Items III and IV, Rome, 19-23 May 1975. WFS 75/5, April 1975.
2 Estimates from FAO and US Departments of Agriculture. *The U.S. and World Agenda for Action 1975*, New York, 1975, pp.196-275.
3 Address by the Secretary for Agriculture Earl L. Butz before the National Association of Farm Broadcasters, 18 October 1974. USDA 2986-74.
4 *Food Aid*, OECD, Paris 1974.
5 James Grant, 'Humanitarian Food Assistance in the New Era of Resource Scarcities', statement submitted to the Senate Subcommittee on Agriculture and Forestry, 4 April 1974, p.9.
6 Mohan Ram, 'The Contributions of the Green Revolution in India', *Le Monde Diplomatique*, October 1974, p.11.
7 James Grant, op. cit.
8 Dan Morgan, 'Political, Charitable Functions Split over US Food Aid Plan', *International Herald Tribune*, 14 December 1974.
9 Dan Morgan, 'Less US Food Aid is found going to the countries needing it most', *Herald Tribune*, 1 February 1975.
10 *World Hunger, Causes and Remedies*, Transnational Institute Report, Amsterdam, October 1974, p.57.
11 'FAO and UNO —World Food Council in Rome', *Neue Zürcher Zeitung*, 23 June 1975.
12 'The Security of the World's Food', *Neue Zürcher Zeitung*, 12 June 1975.
13 Larry Minear, *New Hope for the Hungry?*, New York, 1975, p.58.
14 *World Hunger*, op.cit., p.56.

6 Migration, urbanisation and income inequality

1 Caroline Hutton, 'Aspects of Urban Unemployment in Uganda' in *East African Institute of Social Research,* Conference Papers, January 1966, Kampala, No.358, pp.5-7.

2 *The Poor World Cities* — a special survey by Barbara Ward, *Economist,* 6 December 1969. See also *Socio-Economic Progress in Latin America,* Inter American Development Bank 1968, pp.333-377.

3 *The Impact of Multinational Corporations on Development and on International Relations,* Dept. of Economic and Social Affairs, United Nations, New York, 1974, p.29.

4 E.F. Schumacher, 'Industrialisation through Intermediate Technology' in G.M. Meier (ed.) *Leading Issues in Development Economics,* New York, 1970.

5 Paul Bairoch, *Urban Unemployment in Developing Countries,* ILO 1973.

6 According to Brian R. Mitchell and Phyllis Deane: *Abstract of British historical statistics,* Cambridge, 1962, pp.64-65. By 10-year period, the average percentages are as follows: 1851-60: 4.8, 1861-70: 5.4, 1871-80: 4.0, 1881-90: 5.2, 1891-1900: 4.4, 1901-10: 5.1.

7 According to J. Diczynski: *Die Geschichte der Lage der Arbeiter in Deutschland von 1789 bis in die Gegenward,* Berlin, 1954, vol. 1, Part 2, especially p.80.

8 Robert McNamara, *One Hundred Countries, Two Billion People,* New York, 1973, p.62.

9 The following table prepared by the International Labour Organization while suffering from the weaknesses affecting all such estimates, illustrates the magnitude of the problem. It projects an increase of 170 million in the labour force during the decade 1970-80, with only half as great an increase in the number of fulltime jobs.

Levels of unemployment and underemployment in developing countries excluding China

	1970	1980	1970	1980
	millions		per cent	per cent
Fully employed	504	592	75.3	70.5
Underemployed	130	200	19.4	23.8
			24.7	29.5
Employed	634	792	94.7	94.3
Unemployed	36	48	5.3	5.7
Total	670	840	100.0	100.0

10 David Turnham, The Employment Problem in Less Developed Countries, OECD, 1971, p.1 and pp.93-120.

11 McNamara, op.cit., p.63-64.
12 Economic and Social Progress in Latin America, Inter-American Development Bank, 1968, p.370.
13 J.M. Hume, 'Migrant workers in Europe', *Finance and Development*, vol. 10, no.1, March 1973, pp.2-6.
14 E.J.B. Rose and associates, *Colour and Citizenship, A report on British Race Relations*, Oxford, 1969, p.54.
15 Hugh Brody, *Inishkillane: Change and Decline in the West of Ireland*, London, 1973.
16 Marios Nikolinakos, 'Zur Frage der Auswanderungs-effekte in den Emigrationsländern', *Das Argument*, vol. 13, nos. 9-10, December 1971, pp.782-799.
17 *Migration of Workers as an Element in Employment Policy*, ILO, 1973, D. 22/1973.
18 *Migration and Development — The Case of Algeria*, OECD, 1970.
19 Mahub Ul Haq, 'Employment in the 1970s — A New Perspective', *International Development Review*, April 1971, p.10.
20 McNamara, op.cit., p.103.
21 Albert Fishlow, an unpublished paper shortly to appear in the American Journal of Political Science.
22 McNamara, op.cit., p.103.

7 *Rural development — an alternative development machine*

1 US State Department, *The Employment Problem in Thailand*, September 1972.
2 R.D. Hansen, *The Policies of Mexican Development*, Baltimore, 1971, pp.81, 210.
3 William R. Cline, *Economic Consequences of a Land Reform in Brazil*, Amsterdam, 1970.
4 A. Marzock, *Economic Development and Policies — Case Study of Thailand*, Rotterdam, 1972.
5 E. Owens and R. Shaw, *Development Reconsidered*, London, 1972.
6 R. Meyer, D.W. Adams, N. Rask and P.F. Cidade de Araujo, *Rural Capital Markets and Small Farmers in Brazil, 1960-1972*, Columbus, Ohio, 1973.
7 Gunnar Myrdal, op. cit., p.213.
8 Louis Roussel, 'Measuring rural-urban drift in developing countries: a suggested method', *International Labour Review*, vol. 101, no. 3, March 1970, p.229.
9 R. McNamara, Address to the Board of Governors (World Bank 1973), p.21.
10 A.K. Sen, *Choice of Techniques* (Appendix C), 1960.
11 Owens and Shaw, op. cit., p.116.
12 James Grant, 'Development: The End of Trickle Down', *Foreign Policy*, no. 12, Fall 1973, p.56.
13 McNamara, op.cit., p.24.

8 The Green Revolution

1 *The Death of the Green Revolution,* a Haslemere Group and Third World First Publication, London, 1973.
2 According to Robert d'A. Shaw, *Jobs and Agricultural Development,* Overseas Development Council, Washington, 1971.
3 Research Highlights for 1973, op.cit., p.10. The International Rights Research Institute, Los Baños, Philippines 1974.
4 Barbara Böttger, op. cit., p.63.
5 *The Death of the Green Revolution,* op. cit., p.8.
6 'La Révolution verte', *Service d'information tiers monde,* Berne, Bulletin 1973-4.
7 Robert d'A. Shaw, op.cit., p.44.
8 'Who benefits most from the Green Revolution?' Action UNDP, *Development Forum,* January-February 1975.
9 *The Death of the Green Revolution,* op.cit., p.9.
10 'The Contradictions of the Green Revolution in India', *Le Monde Diplomatique,* October 1974.
11 Erich H. Jacoby, 'The transfer of technology, instrument of neo-capitalism', *Le Monde Diplomatique,* October 1974.
12 'Development in the Villages', Ideas and Realisations, Action for Development/FAO, 1974 2/3, p.14.
13 International Rice Research Institute 1974, Annual Report for 1973, Los Baños, Philippines, p.30.
14 International Rice Research Institute, op. cit., p.26

9 Seven countries

1 *Ujamaa — The Basis of African Socialism,* Julius Nyerere, Dar-es-Salaam, 1962.
2 Goran Hyden, 'Ujamaa, Villagisation and Rural Development in Tanzania', ODI Review, no. 1, 1975.
3 René Dumont, *Problems and Prospects for Rural Development in Bangladesh,* Ford Foundation, Dacca, November 1973, p.51.
4 A good basic description of the project is given in Arthur R. Raper, *Rural Development in Action. The comprehensive experiment at Comilla,* Ithaca and London, 1970. For the view of Akhter Hameed Khan himself see: 'The Comilla Project, a Personal Account', Overseas Liaison Committee, American Council on Education Paper no. 3, March 1974.
5 Bangladesh is divided into 4 Divisions, 17 Districts, 411 Thanas (or counties) and 4,053 Unions.
6 M. Mokammel Haque (Director General of IRDP), 'Comilla Co-operatives and its Replication in Bangladesh', p.10. Unpublished.
7 Dick Wilson, *A Quarter of Mankind,* London, 1966.
8 D. Perkins, 'Looking Inside China — An Economic Appraisal', *Problems of Communism,* May/June 1973; and S. Aziz, 'The

Chinese Approach to Rural Development', *International Development Review*, 1973.

9 M.R. Larsen, 'China's Agriculture under Communism', in Joint Economic Committee of the US Congress, *An Economic Profile of Mainland China*, 1968.

10 S. Aziz, 'The Chinese Approach to Rural Development', *International Development Review*, 1973-4, p.4.

10 The future

1 FAO, 'Assessment of the World Food Situation', Rome, 1974, pp.77-100.

2 A number of alternatives were carefully considered before settling on the base period of 1961-73. As to the starting date, any earlier group of years would have given a period weighted too heavily by conditions of the past; a later starting point would scarcely give a long run of years as the basis for calculating trends and might be too heavily weighted by the very recent past. As to the choice of terminal year (or years) for the base period, both 1970 and 1973 were considered, but after it emerged that in a purely statistical sense the 1971 and 1972 seasons were not untypically bad but rather fell within the to-be-expected limits of fluctuations, it seemed justifiable to prefer 1973 which gave a longer base. Let it be repeated that no base period is ever fully representative; the one used here contains four bad seasons (1965, 1966, 1971 and 1972) out of twelve and therefore the production trends may be a little conservative as far as climatic influences are concerned.

3 We should make the point here that our faith as regards population control is pinned on the social impact of our 5 per cent agricultural growth rate. The evidence presented in chapter 7 suggests that such egalitarian policies offer the best and most effective environment for a sharp decrease in the birth rate.

4 FAO, 'Provisional Indicative World Plan for Agriculture Development', Rome, 1970, vol. 1, pp.12, 25.

5 George Borgstrom, *Too Many: a study of Earth's biological limitations*, London, 1969.

6 ibid.

7 N. Wade, 'International Agricultural Research', *Science*, vol. 188, 9 May 1975, p.586.

8 Lester R. Brown, *By Bread Alone*, New York, 1974.

9 J. Charney of the Massachusetts Institute of Technology, Lecture presented to the Royal Meteorological Society, 1974. See also *Science*, vol. 187, May 1975.

10 'Potential Implications of Trends in World Population, Food Production and Climate', CIA, Washington, 1975.